TOAST

TOAST

BY RAQUEL PELZEL

PHOTOGRAPHS BY
EVAN SUNG

INTRODUCTION

6

FALL

10

WINTER

36

SPRING

64

SUMMER

90

INDEX

118

THIS IS TOAST

Welcome to the modern world of toast, where the bread is flame-kissed, crisped in the toaster, or griddled and then finished with a heap of seasonally inspired toppings. Think of it as a sophisticated evolution of the sandwich and an upgrade from small bites like bruschetta and crostini: as good for breakfast as it is for dessert, as chic for company as it is simple for dinner for one.

Toast can be savory and meaty, calling on serious proteins like a barbecued leg of lamb, or shatteringly crisp honey-glazed fried chicken piled on top of the charred bread. It can also rely on more garden-inspired toppings, like a luscious tomato and avocado salad, or a blistered chile romesco sauce and sautéed mustard greens. Toasts are infinitely amenable, too, and once you begin to explore the world of toasts, you may start putting everything on top of toasted bread—even apple pie! (I'm serious—see page 31.)

Did it all start with innocent avocado toasts, an import from Australia? Beans and toast from England? The Malaysian *kaya* toast topped with coconut jam? Does it matter? Home cooks and chefs alike are turning bread heaped with toppings into a way to offer a new and elevated take on a quick and casual meal. In *Toast*, you'll find fifty ways to take a turn with toast, like topping it with homemade macadamia nut butter infused with cardamom; oven-roasted tomatoes and whipped feta; and even Thanksgiving turkey with fixings; these are just a few ways to change your preconceived notions about what toast can be.

There are lots of ways to crisp the bread for your toast, too; pages 7–8 offer a complete "how to toast" primer. In addition to my takes on toast, you'll find a couple of recipes in each chapter from esteemed and admired chefs and food writers.

So a toast to toasts: May yours be crisp and satisfying with every bite, and may the crumbs always leave a lasting impression!

A TOASTING PRIMER

Some toasts beg for butter, others want olive oil. Some taste best off a grill (barbecue), others are best browned under a broiler (grill) or pan-fried until crispy and golden. For most of the recipes in *Toast*, you can choose whichever method you like. (Please note that the majority of the time, it's best to butter or drizzle the bread with oil before toasting; however, if using a traditional toaster, definitely wait until after the bread is toasted to butter or oil it.) In a few recipes, I suggest a specific method, but, really, it's up to you, so go ahead and own your toast.

BROILED

When I make toast, nine times out of ten, I'll use my broiler (grill). This method of toasting adds the loveliest extra dimension of singed flavor from the broiler element (especially if you have a gas oven—then the toast tastes grill kissed). A grill (barbecue) also does the trick, but in New York City, it's not the most practical approach to cooking for four to five months of the year.

• Drizzle one side of each slice of bread with oil (extra-virgin olive oil or grapeseed oil are my go-to selects) or spread with softened butter, then season with a few pinches of kosher salt.
• Position an oven rack in the top third of the oven, 3–4 inches (7.5–10 cm) from the broiler (grill) element, and preheat to high. If you have an old-school broiler drawer beneath your oven, you can get a better result by setting the baking sheet on top of a muffin tin, thereby elevating the baking sheet to 2–3 inches (5–7.5 cm) from the heating element.
• Set the bread on a foil-lined baking sheet and broil until golden brown, about 2–3 minutes (watch the bread closely as broiler intensities vary—never walk away from food under the broiler!).
• Flip the bread slices and toast the other side until golden brown, another 1–2 minutes.

TOASTER-TOASTED

• Toast the bread, not too dark, then lightly butter or oil after toasting. Compared with other methods, using a toaster often means you'll need to use thinner slices of bread (or even pre-sliced bread) unless you have a wide-slot toaster that offers greater girth for thicker slices.

TOASTER OVEN (MINI OVEN)-TOASTED

- Follow the general directions for the broiler (grill), using the toaster oven's instructions for broiling.

GRILLED (BARBECUED)

- Heat a charcoal or gas grill (barbecue) to medium-high heat.
- Drizzle one side of each slice of bread with oil or spread with butter, then season with salt.
- Grill the bread until toasted and grill-marked on both sides, 1–2 minutes per side.

PAN-FRIED

- Heat 2 tablespoons oil or butter in a large skillet (frying pan)—or 1 tablespoon oil or butter in a medium skillet if toasting in batches—over medium heat. Place the bread in the skillet and set a large heat-safe plate or cake pan on top of the bread—it should fit inside the skillet. If the plate isn't very heavy, weight it down with a few cans of beans or tomatoes. Cook until the bread is golden brown, 2–3 minutes (weighting the bread helps the entire surface area of the crumb come into contact with the hot fat and the hot pan, ensuring a nice, even golden-brown toast).
- Remove the weights and the plate and flip the bread over. Sprinkle the toasted side with salt, then continue to brown the second side, about 1½–2 minutes longer.

SHALLOW-FRIED

- Heat 2 inches (5 cm) of oil in a small or medium skillet (frying pan) over medium-high heat (a larger pan will require extra oil). Add a small cube of bread—if it is immediately surrounded by bubbles, the oil is hot enough.
- Add 1 or 2 bread slices (depending on how big the bread slices are—you don't want to overcrowd the pan) and fry, turning the bread occasionally, until both sides are crisp and golden brown, 4–5 minutes total.
- Transfer the bread to a wire rack set over a baking sheet lined with paper towels or a paper bag. Sprinkle with salt while warm. (Cool the oil, then strain it through cheesecloth [muslin] to reuse another time.)

BREAD BASICS

While working on the toast recipes for this cookbook, I made around four to five *hundred* toasts. Throughout all of this testing and eating, I made some discoveries about bread types and slice thickness. Most toasts are best made using a simple, rustic country-style slice as the base. That said, there are loads of bread styles to consider, and some recipes scream out for a specific bread variety, like the Patty Melt Toast (page 53) on caraway-studded Jewish rye, or the Maple Pear Toast (page 28) with fig jam on a slice of walnut or pecan bread.

BUYING

Remember that the better the bread, the better the toast, so search out a quality bakery or market where the bread is kneaded and baked with care, and sold fresh. When choosing bread, opt for a loaf without lots of tunnels and holes, because there's perhaps nothing more detrimental to the character of a toast than when the toppings fall through the nooks in the bread and onto the plate.

SLICING

A serrated bread knife is your best bet for slicing a loaf without flattening or tearing the bread. When slicing slightly soft day-old (or several-days-old) bread, I find turning the bread on its side and slicing from that perspective prevents further squashing. The ideal thickness of a toast hovers somewhere between ½ inch (1.25 cm) and ¾ inch (2 cm). I tend to lean toward the thicker side and prefer the substantial quality of a crisped bready cushion. If you prefer a thinner bread slice, that's all fine and good, follow your heart—toast is an amenable creature.

STORING

To store a fresh loaf for several days, wrap it in a paper bag and then place the paper bag in a plastic grocery bag to trap moisture so the loaf doesn't get hard and stale. Depending on the bread and its ingredients, the loaf will last anywhere from three to five days, or perhaps longer if it's a slow-fermented bread.

FALL

12   MACADAMIA·CARDAMOM
BUTTER TOAST

15   CHEESY PEPPERONI
BUTTER TOAST

16   ROMESCO TOAST WITH
GARLICKY MUSTARD GREENS

19   CROQUE MONSIEUR TOAST

20   CIDER·GLAZED SQUASH
TOAST WITH MANCHEGO
AND SPICED PECANS

23   WILD MUSHROOM
FOREST TOAST

24   SESAME AND HONEY·BARBECUE
FRIED CHICKEN TOAST

27   THANKSGIVING TOAST

28   MAPLE PEAR TOAST
WITH FIG·SESAME JAM AND
BALSAMIC DRIZZLE

31   DUTCH APPLE PIE TOAST

32   GUEST CHEF:
DEB PERELMAN'S CAULIFLOWER
AND BEER RAREBIT TOAST

35   GUEST CHEF:
HUGH ACHESON'S HAKUREI
TURNIPS, POACHED CHICKEN,
AND APPLE BUTTER TOAST

MACADAMIA-CARDAMOM BUTTER TOAST

Serves 4

Cardamom is, hands down, the spice that captures my heart and imagination. It's exotic and fresh, musky and resinous, and reminds me of strong Turkish coffee, hand-woven rugs, spice bazaars, and kohl-lined eyes. In this ridiculously rich macadamia nut butter, the cardamom and white chocolate give the ground toasted nuts a sweet, decadent vibe. For a toast that is positively sultry, add a few quartered fresh figs or glistening honey-roasted apricot halves (use the roasted pear method on page 28, but substitute apricots for pears and honey for maple syrup).

MACADAMIA-CARDAMOM BUTTER

2 cups (270 g) macadamia nuts
4 ounces (115 g) white chocolate, finely chopped
1½ teaspoons ground cardamom
½ teaspoon kosher (coarse) salt

TOAST

Four ¾-inch (2 cm) thick slices bread
Unsalted butter, softened, for the bread
Kosher (coarse) salt, for the bread

1. **Make the macadamia-cardamom butter:** Preheat the oven to 375°F (190°C/Gas Mark 5).

2. Place the macadamia nuts on a rimmed baking sheet and toast until golden brown, 7–8 minutes, shaking the pan once halfway through toasting. Transfer the nuts to a heat-safe plate to cool.

3. Put the white chocolate in a microwave-safe bowl and microwave on defrost-level heat in 30-second increments, stirring between each, until melted and smooth, 2–3 minutes.

4. In a food processor, combine the toasted macadamia nuts, cardamom, and salt and process until the nuts break down and become a creamy butter, about 1 minute. Add the melted chocolate and process until smooth, about 20 seconds. (The macadamia-cardamom butter will be loose at this point—it firms up after refrigerating.)

5. **Make the toast:** Toast the bread according to the instructions on pages 7–8. Let cool for a minute. To serve, spread each toast with the macadamia-cardamom butter.

CHEESY PEPPERONI
BUTTER TOAST

Serves 4

I have two words that will change your world: pepperoni butter. Just blitz up some soft butter with a chunk of pepperoni. Of course, using good-quality pepperoni makes a difference, and I recommend buying it from a deli as a whole piece rather than presliced, since the latter can get dry ('nduja, a soft spiced-meat mixture, or mortadella are both fantastic too). With fresh mozzarella melted over the top until molten, this toast is like pizza bread 2.0. If you have leftover pepperoni butter, try melting a knob into warmed pasta sauce—it transforms even the plainest red sauce into a nuanced and spectacularly spiced ragu.

PEPPERONI BUTTER

8 tablespoons (115 g) unsalted butter, softened
2 ounces (55 g) unsliced pepperoni,
   cut into ½-inch pieces
½ teaspoon smoked paprika
¼–½ teaspoon red pepper flakes

TOAST

Four ¾-inch (2 cm) thick slices country-style bread
½ pound (225 g) fresh mozzarella cheese,
   cut crosswise into 8 slices
4 tablespoons (¼ cup) roughly chopped or torn
   fresh basil leaves
Kosher (coarse) or flaky salt

1. **Make the pepperoni butter:** In a food processor, combine the butter, pepperoni, smoked paprika, and red pepper flakes and process until well combined. The final mixture should be semi-smooth.

2. **Make the toast:** Spread a generous amount of the pepperoni butter over each slice of bread. Toast according to the broiling instructions on page 7.

3. Heat the broiler (grill) to high and line a baking sheet with foil. Place 2 pieces of mozzarella over each bread slice (overlapping if necessary), set on the baking sheet, and broil until the cheese is melted and browned, 2–3 minutes (watch the cheese closely as broiler intensities vary).

4. To serve, top each toast with 1 tablespoon basil and sprinkle with salt.

ROMESCO TOAST WITH GARLICKY MUSTARD GREENS

Serves 4

In most parts of the United States, sweet summer tomatoes are harvested into October, making a pairing with the season's first wintry greens a natural union. Here, tomatoes find their way into a fried-almond Spanish romesco sauce that gets its bite from medium-sweet dried red chiles and a splash of sherry vinegar. Toss leftover sauce with pasta or use it as a vegetable dip.

ROMESCO SAUCE

1 large tomato, halved horizontally and seeded
⅓ cup (80 ml) extra-virgin olive oil
1 large garlic clove, peeled but whole
1 dried guajillo chile
  (or 1 ancho chile or 2 pasilla chiles)
¼ cup (40 g) lightly toasted almonds
⅓ cup (20 g) baguette cubes (½-inch/2 cm)
1 tablespoon sherry vinegar
1¼ teaspoons kosher (coarse) salt

TOAST

2 tablespoons extra-virgin olive oil,
  plus extra for the bread and for serving
2 garlic cloves, very thinly sliced
¼ teaspoon freshly ground black pepper
6 cups (170 g) roughly chopped mustard greens
  or kale (tough ribs and stems removed)
½ teaspoon plus a few pinches kosher (coarse)
  or flaky salt, for the bread
Four ¾-inch (2 cm) thick slices country-style bread

1. **Make the romesco sauce:** Preheat the broiler (grill) to high. Place the tomato halves on a foil-lined rimmed baking sheet and broil until they start to singe, 6–8 minutes (watch closely as broiler intensities vary). Transfer tomatoes to a food processor.

2. Bring a small pot of water to a boil.

3. In the meantime, in a large skillet (frying pan), combine the olive oil and garlic and set over medium-high heat. Once the garlic starts to sizzle, use tongs to turn often until it begins to turn golden, 1–2 minutes. Add the chile and cook until it puffs out and the garlic is golden brown, 1–2 minutes. Using a slotted spoon, transfer the garlic to the food processor and place the chile in the pot of boiling water, using a plate or glass to submerge.

4. Add the almonds and baguette cubes to the hot oil and fry until golden brown on all sides, 1½–2 minutes. Using a slotted spoon, transfer almonds and bread to the food processor. Pour the oil into a heat-

safe measuring cup.

5. Drain the chile, remove the stem end, and discard the seeds. Add the chile to the food processor along with the vinegar and salt and process until semi-smooth, about 30 seconds. With the machine running, add the reserved olive oil, blending until emulsified, about 1 minute.

6. **Make the toast:** To the same skillet, add 2 tablespoons of the olive oil, the garlic, and black pepper and set it over medium-high heat. Once the garlic becomes golden, after about 30 seconds, add the greens and ½ teaspoon salt. Cook, stirring often, until the greens begin to wilt, 3–4 minutes. Transfer to a fine-mesh sieve or colander set into a sink to drain.

7. Toast the bread according to the instructions on pages 7–8. Top each piece of toast with a few spoonfuls of romesco sauce, followed by mustard greens. Drizzle with more olive oil and sprinkle with flaky salt.

CROQUE MONSIEUR TOAST

Serves 4

This toast was inspired by the croque monsieur served at Harry's Bar in Venice, the legendary bar and restaurant where both the Bellini cocktail and beef carpaccio were invented. Unlike the traditional Parisian version with a béchamel sauce between the layers of ham and Gruyère, at Harry's, the croque is made with an egg yolk that binds a piquant filling of grated Gruyère, Dijon mustard, and Worcestershire sauce. It's like a grilled cheese, all dressed up for a night out.

TOAST

Four ¾-inch (2 cm) thick slices Pullman loaf or
  country-style bread
3 tablespoons extra-virgin olive oil

CROQUE MONSIEUR

4 ounces (1 cup) grated Gruyère cheese
2 ounces (½ cup) grated Emmental cheese
1 egg yolk
2 tablespoons heavy (double) cream,
  plus more if needed
1 teaspoon Worcestershire sauce
¼ teaspoon Dijon mustard
¼ teaspoon kosher (coarse) salt
4 ounces (115 g) sliced Black Forest ham,
  finely chopped

1. **Make the toast:** Drizzle one side of the bread slices with the olive oil. Toast according to the pan-frying method on page 8. Transfer the bread to a foil-lined baking sheet, untoasted side up.

2. **Make the croque monsieur:** In a food processor, combine the Gruyère, Emmental, egg yolk, cream, Worcestershire sauce, mustard, and salt and process until it comes together into a ball, about 20 seconds. Remove the blade from the work bowl and use a spoon to stir the ham into the cheese mixture. Spread the cheese mixture over each slice of bread (if the mixture is too thick add an extra splash of cream). Arrange the toasts on the baking sheet.

3. Adjust an oven rack so it is 6–7 inches (15–18 cm) from the broiler (grill) element and preheat the broiler to high. Broil the toasts until the cheese is golden brown, 3–4 minutes (watch the toast carefully as broiler intensities vary).

CIDER-GLAZED SQUASH TOAST WITH MANCHEGO AND SPICED PECANS

Serves 4 (with leftover squash)

Garam masala is a toasty northern Indian spice blend made from a slew of spices, seeds, and leaves including (but not limited to) cumin, coriander seed, cinnamon, cloves, peppercorns, bay, and even dried rosebuds. The blend is an ideal foil for fall ingredients, like mulled apple cider and roasted squash. Garam masala is available in most supermarkets, or you can make your own house blend by toasting the spices until they are fragrant and then whirling them in a spice grinder until pulverized and fine. In this toast, the garam masala plays off of the warmth of toasted pecans and cider-glazed pan-roasted butternut squash. Thin shards of Manchego cheese, a sharp and salty sheep's milk cheese from Spain, offset the sweetness.

PECANS AND SQUASH

½ cup (50 g) pecan halves
1½ teaspoons canola (rapeseed) oil
2 tablespoons confectioners' (icing) sugar
¾ teaspoon garam masala
¾ teaspoon kosher (coarse) salt
2 tablespoons (30 g) unsalted butter
1½ teaspoons finely chopped fresh rosemary
1 cinnamon stick
½ teaspoon freshly ground black pepper
2 cups (about 12 oz/340 g) butternut squash cubes (½-inch/2 cm)
½ teaspoon ground ginger
⅛ teaspoon cayenne pepper
⅔ cup (155 ml) apple cider, plus more as needed

1. **Make the pecans:** Preheat the oven to 375°F (190°C/Gas Mark 5). Line a rimmed baking sheet with parchment paper.

2. In a medium bowl, toss the pecans with the oil. In a small bowl, whisk together the confectioners' sugar, garam masala, and ¼ teaspoon of the salt. Add to the pecans and toss to combine. Transfer to the baking sheet and toast until fragrant and golden in the middle (remove 1 pecan and break in half to check), 10–12 minutes. Remove from the oven and transfer the pecans to a heat-safe plate to cool. Once cool, roughly chop.

TOAST

Four ¾-inch (2 cm) thick slices country-style bread
Unsalted butter, softened, for the bread
Small wedge of Manchego or other hard sheep's milk cheese (such as Pecorino-Romano)

3. **Make the squash:** In a large skillet (frying pan), melt the butter over medium-high heat. Add the rosemary, cinnamon stick, and pepper. Once they are fragrant, after about 30 seconds, add the squash, ginger, cayenne, and remaining ½ teaspon salt. Reduce the heat to medium and cook the squash until it browns around the edges, stirring occasionally, about 8 minutes. Add the apple cider, reduce the heat to medium-low, and cook, stirring often, until the pan is dry and the squash is tender, about 10 minutes longer (add a splash more apple cider if the pan becomes dry before the squash is tender). Remove from the heat, discard the cinnamon stick, and use a potato masher to smash the squash.

4. **Make the toast:** Toast the bread according to the instructions on pages 7–8. To serve, spoon a generous amount of the smashed squash over each piece of bread, flatten it out, add a few pecan pieces, and finish with some Manchego shards.

WILD MUSHROOM FOREST TOAST

Serves 4

You know what makes my heart happy in the fall? Taking a walk through the woods with fallen leaves crackling underfoot, the smell of pine resin, and wafting wisps of smoke hanging in the air from a wood-burning stove somewhere way off in the distance. This toast brings together that cozy sensation in one edible and delicious package: nutty caramelized onions, rosemary and thyme, and earthy wild mushrooms—it's kind of a tussle, just like the autumn forest floor. The topping is especially magnificent on top of a polenta-style bread or one made with pecorino or black pepper.

ONIONS AND MUSHROOMS

2 tablespoons (30 g) unsalted butter
1 tablespoon extra-virgin olive oil
½ medium yellow onion, halved and thinly sliced
2 teaspoons finely chopped fresh rosemary
1 teaspoon finely chopped fresh thyme
8 ounces (225 g) wild mushrooms
   (such as maitake, chanterelle, or bluefoot),
   stemmed and thinly sliced
1 teaspoon kosher (coarse) salt,
   plus more as needed
1 tablespoon dry vermouth
½ teaspoon freshly ground black pepper

TOAST

3 tablespoons pine nuts
Four ¾-inch (2 cm) thick slices sourdough bread
Extra-virgin olive oil, for the bread
Kosher (coarse) salt, for the bread
1 tablespoon finely chopped fresh flat-leaf parsley

1. **Make the onions and mushrooms:** Heat a large skillet (frying pan) over medium-high heat. Add the butter and olive oil and once the butter melts, add the onions, rosemary, and thyme. Cook, stirring often, until the onions soften and begin to brown, 5–6 minutes. Reduce the heat to medium-low, cover the skillet, and cook, stirring occasionally, until the onions are deeply golden and begin to brown around the edges, 15–20 minutes.

2. Stir in the mushrooms and salt and continue to cook, stirring often, until the mushrooms brown and soften, about 8 minutes. Add the vermouth and pepper, and once the vermouth is completely evaporated and there isn't any pooling liquid in the pan, remove from the heat. Taste and season with more salt if needed.

3. **Make the toast:** In a small skillet (frying pan), toast the pine nuts over medium heat, shaking the pan often, until the nuts are golden brown, 3–5 minutes. Transfer to a heat-safe plate.

4. Toast the bread according to the instructions on pages 7–8. To serve, top with a generous mound of the mushroom mixture and finish with the pine nuts and parsley.

SESAME AND HONEY-BARBECUE FRIED CHICKEN TOAST

Serves 4

This presentation of honey-doused fried chicken lies somewhere between Southern chicken over waffles and Szechuan fried chicken. Coating bread with mayonnaise before toasting forms a super-crisp barrier against the sauce-slicked fried chicken—a trick I also use for the Patty Melt Toast (page 53). Cutting chicken in strips instead of in half offers more crunchy coating in every bite; cutting the thighs in half yields a more equal juicy-interior-to-crunchy-coating ratio.

FRIED CHICKEN

1 cup (240 ml) buttermilk
2½ teaspoons kosher (coarse) salt
½ teaspoon garlic powder
½ teaspoon freshly ground black pepper
½ teaspoon sweet paprika
1½ pounds (680 g) boneless, skinless chicken thighs, halved crosswise or cut into strips
1 cup (125 g) all-purpose (plain) flour
⅓ cup (50 g) cornstarch (cornflour)
3 tablespoons barbecue sauce
2 tablespoons ketchup
2 tablespoons honey
1–2 tablespoons hot sauce
4–5 cups (950 ml–1.2 L) canola (rapeseed) oil
2 tablespoons toasted sesame seeds

1. **Make the fried chicken:** In a medium bowl, whisk together the buttermilk, 2 teaspoons of the salt, the garlic powder, pepper, and paprika. Add the chicken thighs, cover, and refrigerate for 1 hour or overnight.

2. In a large bowl, whisk together the flour, cornstarch, and remaining ½ teaspoon salt. In another large bowl, whisk together the barbecue sauce, ketchup, honey, and hot sauce and set aside.

3. Remove the chicken from the buttermilk (discard the marinade). Add the chicken to the flour mixture and turn to coat. Set aside while you heat the oil.

TOAST

Four slices sandwich bread
3 tablespoons mayonnaise, for the bread
Kosher (coarse) salt, for the bread

4. Set a wire rack over a baking sheet lined with paper towels or paper bag. In a large, deep, heavy-bottomed skillet (frying pan), heat the oil over medium-high heat until an instant-read thermometer reads between 360°F (180°C) and 365°F (185°C). Add half of the chicken pieces and fry until both sides are golden brown and the chicken is cooked through, 4–5 minutes per side. Use tongs to transfer the chicken to the wire rack to drain and fry the remaining chicken.

5. **Make the toast:** Spread the bread slices with the mayonnaise and sprinkle with salt. Toast according to the broiler or pan-frying instructions on pages 7–8 (note that mayonnaise browns faster than butter or oil, so keep a close eye on the toast to make sure it doesn't burn; if pan-frying, you don't need to melt butter or add oil to the pan first—the mayo coating on the bread is sufficient for browning).

6. Place the fried chicken in the bowl with the barbecue sauce mixture and toss to coat. Sprinkle with sesame seeds, place 1 or 2 chicken pieces on top of each piece of toast, and serve.

THANKSGIVING
TOAST

Serves 4

Thanksgiving. Leftovers. For Americans, these two words are so eagerly awaited all year long. Even if you're missing any of the elements below, it's simple to create a workaround. You can use stuffing instead of mashed potatoes; applesauce in place of cranberries; or cooked vegetables in place of turkey for a vegetarian version. It'll be like having Thanksgiving all over again but with a fraction of the work and all of the payoff!

---

5 tablespoons (70 g) unsalted butter
4 fresh sage leaves, roughly chopped
1 garlic clove, thinly sliced
1¼ cups (285 g) shredded turkey meat (preferably a combination of white and dark meat)
Kosher (coarse) salt
Four ¾-inch (2 cm) thick slices bread

¾ cup (180 g) mashed potatoes (warmed in the microwave if cold)
¼ cup (about 60 g) grated cheese (such as Cheddar, Swiss, or Gouda)
½ cup (120 ml) cranberry sauce or relish
½ cup (120 ml) gravy (optional)
1 tablespoon finely chopped fresh chives

---

1. Place the butter, sage, and garlic in a microwave-safe bowl and microwave in 20-second increments on high until the butter is melted and the sage and garlic are fragrant, up to 1½ minutes.

2. Measure out 2 tablespoons of the sage butter and transfer to a medium skillet (frying pan) set over medium heat. Add the turkey and cook, stirring often, until the turkey is somewhat crispy and warmed through, no more than 3–4 minutes (take care not to dry out the turkey). Season with a few pinches of salt and set aside.

3. Preheat the broiler (grill) to high. Brush the remaining 3 tablespoons of the sage butter over the bread and arrange on a baking sheet. Toast according to the broiler method on page 7. Leave the broiler on.

4. In a small bowl, stir together the mashed potatoes and cheese. Spread the cranberry sauce over the buttered side of each toast. Divide the cheesy mashed potatoes over the cranberry sauce and return the toasts to the broiler until the potatoes are lightly browned on top, 30 seconds–1 minute (watch the potatoes closely as broiler intensities vary).

5. To serve, mound the turkey on top of the potatoes, pour the gravy over the top (if using), and sprinkle with chives.

MAPLE PEAR TOAST WITH FIG-SESAME JAM AND BALSAMIC DRIZZLE

Serves 4

Fruit, acid, cheese, bread: This toast combines all the best parts of a cheese plate into one toast. The pears are roasted with brown sugar and maple syrup until they become caramelized and tender. They are layered over a swipe of fig jam that surprises with the nutty crunch of toasted sesame seeds. Reduced balsamic vinegar adds a syrupy tang, and shards of crystalline Parmigiano-Reggiano counter the sweetness.

MAPLE PEARS

2 tablespoons lightly packed light brown sugar
2 tablespoons maple syrup
2 pinches of kosher (coarse) salt
2 semi-firm Bartlett (Williams) pears, halved, cored, and each half sliced lengthwise into sixths

TOAST

¼ cup (60 ml) balsamic vinegar
1 tablespoon white sesame seeds, toasted
4 tablespoons (¼ cup) fig jam
Four ¾-inch (2 cm) thick slices fruit-and-nut bread
Unsalted butter, softened, for the bread
Small wedge of Parmigiano-Reggiano cheese

1. **Make the maple pears:** Preheat the oven to 400°F (200°C/Gas Mark 6). Line a rimmed baking sheet with parchment paper.

2. In a medium bowl, stir together the brown sugar, maple syrup, and salt. Add the pear slices and gently toss to coat. Place the pears on the baking sheet and roast until the pears are tender and starting to brown around the edges, 18–20 minutes. Remove from the oven, gently turn the pears over, and set aside to cool.

3. **Make the toast:** In a small saucepan, simmer the vinegar over medium heat until it has reduced by about half and is thick and syrupy, 3–5 minutes.

(It will continue to thicken as it cools; if it gets too thick to drizzle, heat for a few seconds in the microwave.) In a small bowl, stir the sesame seeds into the fig jam.

4. Toast the bread according to the instructions on pages 7–8.

5. Using a vegetable peeler, shave ribbons from the wedge of Parmigiano-Reggiano. Spread some fig jam over each piece of toast, then layer a few pear slices over the jam (you may have leftover pears if your bread slices are small). Drizzle with the balsamic reduction and serve topped with the shaved cheese.

DUTCH APPLE PIE TOAST

Serves 4

Sometimes you just want all the pleasure of apple pie without any of the work of making pie dough. That's how I came up with the idea of topping a piece of buttery toast with warm-spiced sautéed apples and a nugget-y streusel pie topping. The toast stands in for the bottom crust—and I promise, you'll barely miss it.

APPLES AND STREUSEL

2 Granny Smith apples (or other crisp-tart apples), peeled, cored, and chopped into ½-inch (1 cm) pieces
4 tablespoons (¼ cup) dried cranberries
3 tablespoons granulated sugar
1 tablespoon fresh lemon juice
½ teaspoon ground cinnamon
¼ teaspoon kosher (coarse) salt
6 tablespoons (85 g) unsalted butter
2 tablespoons heavy (double) cream
⅔ cup (40 g) all-purpose (plain) flour
2 tablespoons light brown sugar
2 teaspoons cornmeal

TOAST

Four ¾-inch (2 cm) thick slices country-style bread
Unsalted butter, softened, for the bread
Confectioners' (icing) sugar

1. **Make the apples and streusel:** In a medium bowl, stir together the apples, cranberries, 2 tablespoons of the granulated sugar, the lemon juice, cinnamon, and ⅛ teaspoon of the salt.

2. In a medium saucepan, melt 2 tablespoons of the butter over medium-high heat. Add the apple mixture, reduce the heat to medium, and cook, stirring occasionally, until the juices from the apples have mostly evaporated, about 8 minutes. Stir in the cream and continue to cook until the apples are very soft and can be easily mashed, 4–5 minutes. Remove from the heat and using a fork, smash about half of the apples.

3. While the apples simmer, preheat the oven to 350°F (180°C/Gas Mark 4). Line a rimmed baking sheet with parchment paper.

4. In a medium bowl, whisk together the flour, brown sugar, cornmeal, and remaining 1 tablespoon granulated sugar and ⅛ teaspoon salt. Melt the remaining 4 tablespoons (¼ cup) butter and drizzle it over the flour mixture, using a fork to stir until the streusel forms knobby bits. Transfer the streusel to the baking sheet and bake until it is golden brown, 8–10 minutes. Remove the streusel from the oven.

5. **Make the toast:** Toast the bread according to the instruc-tions on pages 7–8. To serve, spoon the apples over the toast and top with a handful of streusel, pressing down on the streusel to get it to stick. Dust with confectioners' sugar and serve.

CAULIFLOWER AND BEER RAREBIT TOAST

New York City | Serves 4

Deb Perelman, of the popular *Smitten Kitchen* blog and cookbook, combined two cheesy obsessions of hers into one English pub–style toast: cauliflower and rarebit. The béchamel for the rarebit is made with extra-sharp Cheddar and stout beer instead of the traditional milk. The molten sauce is ladled over cauliflower-topped bread (roasting the cauliflower at 400°F [200°C/Gas Mark 6] with a couple of tablespoons of oil for about 20 minutes is especially nice if you have the time), resulting in one incredibly comforting, cozy toast.

CAULIFLOWER AND CHEESE SAUCE

1 small head cauliflower, cut into bite-size florets
2½ teaspoons kosher (coarse) salt
3 tablespoons (45 g) unsalted butter
3 tablespoons all-purpose (plain) flour
2 teaspoons Dijon mustard or mustard powder
¼ teaspoon cayenne pepper
1½ cups (12 fl oz/355 ml) porter or stout beer
1 teaspoon Worcestershire sauce,
   plus extra for serving
1½ cups (about 6 oz/170 g) grated extra-sharp
   Cheddar cheese

1. **Make the cauliflower:** Bring a saucepan of water to a boil. Add the cauliflower and 2 teaspoons of the salt and cook until the cauliflower is just tender, 4–5 minutes. Drain, then turn the cauliflower out onto a tea towel to cool.

2. **Make the cheese sauce**: In the saucepan used for the cauliflower, melt the butter over medium-high heat. Add the flour and whisk constantly for 1 minute. Whisk in the mustard and cayenne. Drizzle in the beer in a slow stream, whisking constantly to ensure the mixture remains smooth. Add the Worcestershire sauce and the remaining ½ teaspoon salt, and stir using a wooden spoon until the mixture

TOAST

Four ¾-inch (2 cm) thick slices rye bread
Fresh flat-leaf parsley (optional)

thickens a bit, 30 seconds–1 minute. Add the Cheddar, a little at a time, letting each addition melt before adding the next. Once all of the cheese is added, remove from the heat, taste, and adjust the seasonings if needed. Set aside to cool slightly.

3. **Make the toast:** While the sauce cools, preheat the broiler (grill) to high. Line a rimmed baking sheet with foil. Arrange the bread on the sheet and broil until golden brown on both sides, 1½–2 minutes per side.

4. To serve, top each toast with a few cauliflower florets. Ladle a generous amount of the cheese sauce over each toast, splash with a few shakes of Worcestershire, and serve with parsley, if desired.

HAKUREI TURNIPS, POACHED CHICKEN, AND APPLE BUTTER TOAST

Georgia | Serves 4

Sweet Hakurei turnips, originally from Japan, can be found at farmers' markets from early spring throughout the fall. Georgia-based chef Hugh Acheson—of Five & Ten, The National, Empire State South, and The Florence—poaches chicken thighs and the turnips in chicken stock before piling them on olive oil–fried bread. Acheson sautés the turnip greens with garlic and uses them to top the toast.

POACHED CHICKEN AND TURNIPS

2 tablespoons (30 g) unsalted butter
½ small yellow onion, very finely chopped
½ celery stalk, very finely chopped
1 sprig fresh thyme
2 bay leaves
2 cups (475 ml) chicken stock or broth
2 bone-in, skinless chicken thighs
½ teaspoon kosher (coarse) salt
8 small Hakurei turnips, unpeeled, greens reserved, turnips quartered

1. **Poach the chicken and turnips:** In a medium pot, melt the butter over medium heat. Add the onion and celery and cook, stirring, until the onion softens, about 5 minutes. Add the thyme, bay leaves, and chicken stock and bring to a simmer (the temperature of the liquid should be 180°F/85°C).

2. Season the chicken with salt and add to the pot. Cover and poach until the chicken is tender and cooked through, about 20 minutes. Remove the chicken from the stock and set aside to cool.

3. Add the turnips to the poaching liquid, reduce the heat to medium-low, and cook until tender, about 7 minutes. Drain and set aside.

TOAST

4 tablespoons (¼ cup) extra-virgin olive oil
Four ¾-inch (2 cm) thick slices pain de campagne
Reserved Hakurei turnip greens
½ teaspoon kosher (coarse) salt
4 tablespoons apple butter
½ cup (115 g) crumbled firm farmer cheese, quark, or cow's milk feta
¼ cup (55 g) crushed Marcona almonds

4. **Make the toast:** In a heavy-bottomed skillet, heat the olive oil over medium-high heat until almost smoking, 2½–3 minutes. Add 2 of the bread slices and fry on each side until golden brown, about 2 minutes per side. Transfer to a paper towel-lined plate and repeat with the remaining bread.

5. Pour off all but 1 tablespoon of the olive oil in the skillet, add the reserved turnip greens, and cook until they start to wilt, about 1 minute. Season with salt and add the poached turnips, tossing them with the greens. Remove from the heat. Pull the chicken from the bones and shred the meat, then toss with the turnips and greens to combine.

6. Spread the apple butter on the toasts. Mound the chicken, turnip, and greens mixture on top. Sprinkle with farmer cheese and almonds.

WINTER

38   BEST CINNAMON TOAST

41   ROASTED BEETS ON TOAST WITH
      LABNEH AND SAFFRON HONEY

42   SMASHED TOT AND EGG TOAST

45   LENTIL, BACON, AND
      CABBAGE TOAST

46   BOMBAY BUBBLE AND
      SQUEAK TOAST

49   THREE-CHEESE SPINACH-
      ARTICHOKE TOAST

50   ROASTED TOMATO AND
      FETA CREAM TOAST

53   PATTY MELT TOAST

54   ROAST BEEF, RÉMOULADE, AND
      FRIED ONIONS SMØRREBRØD

57   CRANBERRY UPSIDE-DOWN
      TOAST

58   LEMONGRASS KIWI TOAST
      WITH HONEY CREAM

61   GUEST CHEF:
      SUVIR SARAN'S SPICY
      LOBSTER BALCHAO TOAST

62   GUEST CHEF:
      FERGUS HENDERSON'S BEEF
      MINCE ON TOAST

BEST CINNAMON TOAST

Serves 4

My mother is not a great cook. That said, cinnamon toast is hard to mess up, and it truly is one of her best "home cooked" dishes, so it owns a small corner of my heart. Here, I take the toast a couple of steps further: I soak buttered and toasted bread in cinnamon sugar syrup, which gives the toast an almost custardy quality. Then I press the sticky side of the bread into cinnamon sugar and fry the bread in butter so the sugar caramelizes around the edges and becomes almost candy-like.

CINNAMON SYRUP

½ cup (100 g) sugar
3 cinnamon sticks

TOAST

Four ¾-inch (2 cm) thick slices Pullman loaf or
 whole wheat bread
6 tablespoons (85 g) unsalted butter, softened
3 tablespoons sugar
2 teaspoons ground cinnamon
Confectioners' (icing) sugar (optional)

1. **Make the cinnamon syrup:** In a small saucepan, combine the sugar, cinnamon sticks, and ½ cup (120 ml) water and bring to a boil over high heat, stirring often to dissolve the sugar. Reduce the heat to medium-low and simmer until the cinnamon is very fragrant, about 5 minutes. Remove from the heat and set aside to cool (the syrup can be refrigerated for up to 3 weeks).

2. **Make the toast:** Using 3–4 tablespoons of the butter, coat both sides of each piece of bread. Toast according to the broiler or pan-frying instructions on pages 7–8. Brush a generous amount of cinnamon syrup over one side of each slice (add enough syrup to saturate the bread without making it soggy).

3. In a small bowl, mix the sugar with the cinnamon until combined, then transfer all but 2 teaspoons of it to a plate. Dip each piece of toast, syrup side down, in the cinnamon sugar.

4. In a large skillet (frying pan), melt the remaining 2–3 tablespoons butter over medium-high heat. Reduce the heat to medium and place the toast, sugared side down, in the skillet. Set a large heat-safe plate on top of the toast to press it down (place one or two cans of beans on top to weight it down). Cook until the edges of the bread are caramelized and the sugar is completely melted and glistening across the surface of the bread, 3–4 minutes.

5. Serve each slice of toast caramelized side up and sprinkled with some of the reserved cinnamon sugar and, if desired, confectioners' sugar.

ROASTED BEETS ON TOAST WITH LABNEH AND SAFFRON HONEY

Serves 4

Labneh is a Lebanese strained yogurt that is quite rich and tastes almost like a sour cream/crème fraîche hybrid. It comes fresh in a tub, like yogurt, or as balls preserved in a jar of olive oil, almost like cheese. Here, I use the creamy version spooned over toast and paired with stunning roasted beets (beetroots) and saffron-infused honey. Toasted pistachios and chopped fresh mint add a pretty bright color and nice crunch.

SAFFRON HONEY AND ROASTED BEETS

½ teaspoon saffron threads
½ cup (120 ml) honey
¼ teaspoon plus a pinch of kosher (coarse) salt
3 medium beets (beetroots), ends trimmed
2 tablespoons extra-virgin olive oil
2 teaspoons finely chopped fresh mint leaves
Freshly ground black pepper

TOAST

Four ¾-inch (2 cm) thick slices country-style bread
Extra-virgin olive oil, for the bread
Kosher (coarse) salt, for the bread
1 cup (240 ml) labneh (Lebanese-style) yogurt
  or plain Greek yogurt
4 tablespoons (¼ cup) toasted and roughly
  chopped pistachios
Flaky salt

1. **Make the saffron honey:** Toast the saffron in a small skillet (frying pan) over medium heat, shaking the pan often, until the saffron is fragrant, 30 seconds–1 minute. Transfer the saffron to a small dish and use the back of a teaspoon to crush it into a fine powder. Add the honey to the skillet and bring it to a simmer over medium heat. Stir in the saffron and a pinch of salt, remove from the heat, and set aside.

2. **Roast the beets:** Preheat the oven to 375°F (190°C/Gas Mark 5). Set each beet in a large square of foil and drizzle 1 teaspoon of the oil over the top of each beet. Wrap the beets in the foil, place them on a rimmed baking sheet, and roast until a paring knife easily slides into the center of the largest beet, about 1 hour. Remove from the oven and set aside for 20 minutes before unwrapping. Once the beets are cool enough to handle, peel them and chop into bite-size pieces. Toss the beets with 1 tablespoon of the oil, the mint leaves, ¼ teaspoon of salt, and the pepper and set aside.

3. **Make the toast:** Toast the bread according to the instructions on pages 7–8. Let the toasts cool for a few minutes before topping. To serve, spread each toast with labneh. Top with beets, pistachios, a generous drizzle of saffron honey, and flaky salt.

SMASHED TOT
AND EGG TOAST

Serves 4

Crispy baked Tater Tots (little potato croquettes) are a love marriage between French fries and hash browns. They're deeply satisfying smashed on buttery toast and topped with a fried egg. I'm a ketchup lover, so I zigzag it over the top like a Pollock painting. You can also try Sriracha, salsa, or hot sauce. This is the toast I crave after an epic night out, when I wake up hungry and in need of sustenance. Try it—you'll see.

TATER TOTS

8 ounces (225 g) frozen Tater Tots (potato croquettes)
1 tablespoon grapeseed oil

TOAST

Four ¾-inch (2 cm) thick slices country-style bread or Pullman loaf
1 tablespoon (15 g) unsalted butter, softened, plus extra for the bread
4 eggs
Kosher (coarse) salt and freshly ground black pepper
Ketchup, salsa, Sriracha, or hot sauce
Flaky salt

1. **Bake the Tater Tots:** Preheat the oven to the temperature suggested on the package of Tater Tots. In a medium bowl, toss the Tater Tots with the oil (this helps make them extra crispy) and place them on a rimmed baking sheet. Bake according to the package directions.

2. **Make the toast:** Follow the instructions on page 8 to pan-fry the bread. Transfer each piece of toast to a plate. Divide the Tater Tots among the toasts, using a fork to smash them down.

3. Heat the remaining 1 tablespoon butter in the same skillet (frying pan) over medium-high heat. Crack the eggs into the skillet, season with salt and pepper, and cook until the whites are set and the yolks are still runny, 3–4 minutes. To serve, set an egg on top of each toast, stripe with ketchup, and sprinkle with a few pinches of flaky salt.

LENTIL, BACON, AND CABBAGE TOAST

Serves 4

Lentils are a weekly staple in my house. They are inexpensive and packed with protein, fiber, and iron. Here, I use duck bacon (pork bacon works too) to give the meaty lentils an even heartier taste, but you could easily lose the bacon for a vegetarian-friendly meal (or use vegetarian bacon instead). Thin ruffles of cabbage lighten the overall dish—add a poached or fried egg to any leftovers and you have total breakfast bliss.

LENTILS

2 tablespoons extra-virgin olive oil
5 slices (rashers) bacon (preferably duck bacon),
   thinly sliced crosswise
4 medium shallots, finely chopped
½ teaspoon freshly ground black pepper
2 medium garlic cloves, finely chopped
2½ cups thinly sliced green (white) cabbage
   (about ¼ of a medium head)
1½ teaspoons finely chopped fresh thyme
1 teaspoon kosher (coarse) salt
¾ cup (165 g) green French lentils (Puy lentils),
   rinsed
½ cup (120 ml) dry white wine
1 tablespoon (15 g) unsalted butter

TOAST

Four ¾-inch (2 cm) thick slices country-style bread
Extra-virgin olive oil, for the bread,
   plus extra for serving
Kosher (coarse) salt, for the bread
2 scallions (spring onions), thinly sliced

1. **Make the lentils:** In a large, deep skillet (frying pan), heat the olive oil over medium heat. Add the bacon and cook until the fat is rendered and the bacon is crisp, 5–6 minutes. Using a slotted spoon, transfer it to a plate and set aside. Add the shallots and pepper to the skillet and cook until the shallots begin to soften, about 1 minute. Stir in the garlic and cook until it is fragrant, 30 seconds. Stir in the cabbage, thyme, and salt and cook, stirring occasionally, until the cabbage begins to stick to the pan, 7–8 minutes.

2. Stir in the lentils and wine. Increase the heat to high and simmer, stirring occasionally, until all of the wine is evaporated, 2–3 minutes. Add 1½ cups (355 ml) water and bring to a boil. Reduce the heat to medium-low, cover, and cook until the lentils are tender, about 50 minutes. Uncover and stir in the butter.

3. **Make the toast:** Toast the bread according to the instructions on pages 7–8. To serve, cover each piece of toast with lentils. Sprinkle the reserved bacon and scallions on top and drizzle with olive oil.

BOMBAY BUBBLE AND SQUEAK TOAST

Serves 4

There are loads of ingenious ways to use up leftover mashed potatoes, but one of the most innovative takes has to be England's bubble and squeak, named for the noises the mashed potatoes make as they pan-fry in melted butter. Because the Brits love their curry (and so do I), I add curry powder and chopped cilantro to the cabbage, carrots, and onions for a South Indian vibe. The patties are fried and then smashed onto sweet-and-spicy mango chutney–swiped toast. If you like things with a knock of heat, add some fresh, finely chopped jalapeño to the potato mixture.

BUBBLE AND SQUEAK

¼ small head green (white) cabbage, cut into
   ½-inch (1 cm) wide strips
2 medium carrots, sliced crosswise into ½-inch
   (1.25 cm) rounds
½ medium red onion, halved and thinly sliced
2 tablespoons extra-virgin olive oil
1 teaspoon curry powder
2¼ teaspoons kosher (coarse) salt
2 medium potatoes (such as Yukon Gold or Bintje),
   peeled and chopped into ½-inch (1.25 cm) pieces
1 teaspoon ground turmeric
¼ cup whole (full-fat) milk
3 tablespoons (45 g) unsalted butter, softened
2 tablespoons finely chopped fresh cilantro

TOAST

Four ¾-inch (2 cm) thick slices country-style bread
Grapeseed oil, for the bread
Kosher (coarse) salt, for the bread
4 tablespoons (¼ cup) spicy mango chutney

1. **Make the bubble and squeak:** Preheat the oven to 400°F (200°C/Gas Mark 6). In a bowl, toss together the cabbage, carrots, onion, oil, curry powder, and ½ teaspoon of the salt. Transfer the mixture to a rimmed baking sheet. Roast until the cabbage and onions are browned and the carrots are tender, 25–30 minutes, stirring once halfway through roasting.

2. While the vegetables roast, in a medium saucepan, combine the potatoes and 1 teaspoon of the salt, and cover with water. Bring to a boil, add the turmeric, and cook until the potatoes are tender, 10–12 minutes. Drain the potatoes.

3. Add the milk to the saucepan and bring it to a simmer over medium-high heat. Once it starts to bubble, add the potatoes and remove from the heat. Using a potato masher or fork, smash the potatoes, then add 2 tablespoons (30 g) of the butter and the remaining salt, stirring and smashing until the butter is completely incorporated. Stir in the roasted vegetables and cilantro.

4. Shape the potato mixture into 4 patties, flattening them out slightly. In a large nonstick skillet (frying pan), melt the remaining 1 tablespoon butter over medium-high heat. Add the potato patties and fry until browned on both sides, 3–4 minutes total.

5. **Make the toast:** Toast the bread according to the instructions on pages 7–8. To serve, spread each toast with 1 tablespoon mango chutney. Top with a potato patty, smashing it slightly onto the bread.

THREE·CHEESE
SPINACH·ARTICHOKE
TOAST

Serves 4

Come the winter holiday season, I'm pretty much guaranteed to attend *at least* one party where artichoke dip is served. This tangy version is chock-full of artichokes and spinach, as well as Gouda, Cheddar, and Parmigiano-Reggiano cheeses. Since artichoke dip is usually served alongside bread, it makes sense to consolidate matters for your guests and serve this up in a ready-to-eat format.

SPINACH·ARTICHOKE DIP

1 tablespoon extra-virgin olive oil
½ red onion, finely chopped
½ teaspoon plus a pinch kosher (coarse) salt
½ cup (120 ml) sour cream
4 tablespoons (¼ cup) mayonnaise
⅓ cup (85 g) grated Gouda cheese
⅓ cup (85 g) grated mild Cheddar cheese
⅓ cup plus 2 tablespoons (115 g) finely grated
  Parmigiano-Reggiano cheese
Finely grated zest of 1 lemon
½ teaspoon garlic powder
3 marinated artichoke hearts, roughly chopped
4 cups (115 g) roughly chopped baby spinach

TOAST

Four ¾-inch (2 cm) thick slices country-style bread
Extra-virgin olive oil, for the bread
Kosher (coarse) salt, for the bread
1 tablespoon finely chopped fresh chives

1. **Make the spinach-artichoke dip:** Preheat the oven to 375°F (190°C/Gas Mark 5).

2. In a medium skillet (frying pan), heat the olive oil over medium-high heat. Add the onion and a pinch of salt and cook, stirring occasionally, until the onion starts to brown, 3–4 minutes.

3. Scrape the onion into a medium bowl and stir in the sour cream, mayonnaise, Gouda, Cheddar, 2 tablespoons (30 g) of the Parmigiano-Reggiano, the lemon zest, garlic powder, and remaining ½ teaspoon salt. Stir in the artichokes and spinach and

transfer the mixture to a small baking dish (the dip should fill the baking dish by about 1–1½ inches [2.5–4 cm] deep). Sprinkle the top with the remaining Parmigiano-Reggiano and bake until the mixture is bubbling and starting to brown, about 20 minutes. Remove from the oven and set aside to cool for 20 minutes.

4. **Make the toast:** Toast the bread according to the instructions on pages 7–8. To serve, top each toast with some of the artichoke mixture and sprinkle with chives.

ROASTED TOMATO AND FETA CREAM TOAST

Serves 4

Out-of-season tomatoes are generally a sad lot, but roasting them initiates an alchemic series of events where the essence of the tomatoes concentrates and sweetens, and the tomatoes become super juicy. Paired with a rich and creamy feta sauce, this toast is pure decadence. Buy the best dried oregano you can find, and if it has been sitting in your pantry for longer than a year, take the plunge and buy a new bottle. Crushing the herbs between your fingers before sprinkling releases their essential oils—and makes a big difference when it comes to the freshest, brightest taste.

ROASTED TOMATOES AND FETA CREAM

4 plum tomatoes, cored and halved lengthwise
½ teaspoon sweet paprika
½ teaspoon freshly ground black pepper
½ teaspoon kosher (coarse) salt
1 tablespoon extra-virgin olive oil
½ cup (75 g) crumbled feta cheese
3 tablespoons plain Greek yogurt
2 tablespoons mayonnaise
1 medium garlic clove, very finely chopped
½ teaspoon dried oregano

TOAST

Four ¾-inch (2 cm) thick slices country-style bread
Extra-virgin olive oil for the bread,
   plus extra for drizzling
Kosher (coarse) salt, for the bread
Flaky salt
Freshly ground black pepper

1. **Make the tomatoes and feta cream:** Preheat the oven to 375°F (190°C/Gas Mark 5). Line a rimmed baking sheet with parchment paper.

2. Place the tomatoes cut side up on the baking sheet. In a small bowl, mix together the paprika, pepper, and ¼ teaspoon of the salt. Drizzle the tomatoes with the oil and sprinkle with the paprika mixture. Roast until the juices are bubbling and the tomatoes are very tender and browned on the bottom, 50 minutes–1 hour. Remove from the oven and set aside to cool.

3. In a medium bowl, stir together the feta, yogurt, mayonnaise, garlic, oregano, and remaining ¼ teaspoon salt.

4. **Make the toast:** Toast the bread according to the instructions on pages 7–8. To serve, top each toast with a generous spoonful of the feta cream, then add a tomato, drizzle with olive oil, and sprinkle with a pinch of flaky salt and a few grinds of pepper.

PATTY MELT TOAST

Serves 4

Chefs are having a bit of a love affair with the patty melt, the American diner standard of a burger topped with caramelized onions and melted Swiss, sandwiched between two butter-griddled slices of rye bread. Here, it is re-created as a toast, or, really, an open-face burger. Toasted and finely ground caraway seeds bring the patty's flavor to the next level, but if you don't have the time, you can skip the toasting step. Honestly, though, it really is worth it, and just takes a minute or two over medium heat in a dry skillet.

BEEF AND ONIONS

1 tablespoon Worcestershire sauce
2 teaspoons Dijon mustard
2¼ teaspoons kosher (coarse) salt
1 teaspoon caraway seeds, toasted
  and finely ground
½ teaspoon freshly ground black pepper
¼ teaspoon garlic powder
1 pound (455 g) ground (minced) sirloin
2 tablespoons (30 g) unsalted butter
1 medium yellow onion, halved and thinly sliced

TOAST

Four ¾-inch (2 cm) thick slices rye bread
3 tablespoons mayonnaise, for the bread
Kosher (coarse) salt, for the bread
1 cup (110 g) grated Gruyère or Swiss cheese
  (or 8 slices Gruyère or Swiss)

1. **Make the beef and onions:** In a medium bowl, whisk together the Worcestershire sauce, mustard, 1¼ teaspoons of the salt, caraway, pepper, and garlic powder. Add the sirloin and toss the mixture together to combine. Divide it into 4 equal portions and shape each into a patty ½-inch (1.25 cm) thick.

2. In a large skillet (frying pan), melt the butter over medium-high heat. Add the onion and the remaining 1 teaspoon salt and cook, stirring often, until the onion is soft and browned, 6–8 minutes. Transfer to a small plate and set aside.

3. Add the patties to the skillet and cook until browned on both sides and cooked to medium-rare to medium, 5–6 minutes total.

4. **Make the toast:** Spread one side of the bread slices with the mayonnaise and sprinkle with salt. Broil or pan-fry according to the instructions on pages 7–8 (if pan-frying, you don't need to melt the butter or add oil to the pan before adding the bread—the mayo on the bread is more than enough to get the toast golden brown). Set a patty on each piece of toast and top with cheese. Preheat the broiler (grill) to high and broil the toasts until the cheese is melted and browned, 2–3 minutes. To serve, top with a tangle of fried onions.

ROAST BEEF, RÉMOULADE, AND FRIED ONIONS SMØRREBRØD

Serves 4 (with leftover rémoulade)

Hot/cold, crispy/creamy, tangy/rich: These are the dualities of the classic *smørrebrød* roast beef and rémoulade toast with crackling fried onions. Rémoulade, which is similar to American tartar sauce, gets a yellow tint from a dash of turmeric or curry powder. Here, I go with the former to keep the flavor more neutral; but for a taste of the subcontinent, swap in curry powder instead.

RÉMOULADE

½ cup (120 ml) mayonnaise
1 medium shallot, very finely chopped
1 tablespoon grainy mustard
1 tablespoon fresh lemon juice
1 tablespoon finely chopped fresh flat-leaf parsley
1 tablespoon drained capers, rinsed and roughly chopped
1 tablespoon roughly chopped cornichon pickles
¼ teaspoon ground turmeric or curry powder
¼ teaspoon kosher (coarse) salt

TOAST

Four ¾-inch (2 cm) thick slices rye or pumpernickel bread
Extra-virgin olive oil, for the bread
¼ teaspoon plus a pinch kosher (coarse) salt
4–6 cups (950 ml–1.4 L) canola (rapeseed) oil
4 tablespoons (¼ cup) all-purpose (plain) flour
¼ teaspoon freshly ground black pepper
1 large yellow onion, cut crosswise into slices ¼-inch (0.5 cm) thick and separated into rings
12 slices roast beef
Roughly chopped fresh flat-leaf parsley

1. **Make the rémoulade:** In a small bowl, whisk together the mayonnaise, shallot, mustard, lemon juice, parsley, capers, pickles, turmeric, and salt. Cover and refrigerate.

2. **Make the toast:** Toast the bread according to the instructions on pages 7–8.

3. Pour enough canola oil into a medium saucepan to come up 2–3 inches (5–7.5 cm). Heat the oil over medium-high heat until it reaches 350°F (180°C) on an instant-read thermometer. In a medium bowl, combine the flour, ¼ teaspoon salt, and the pepper. Add the onion rings and toss to coat. Fry the onions in batches, adding a handful at a time, and turning occasionally with chopsticks or a slotted spoon, until golden brown and crisp, 4–5 minutes. Let the oil heat back up to 350°F (180°C) before adding the next batch. Using a slotted spoon or a spider, transfer the onions to a plate lined with paper towels and season with a pinch of salt.

4. Top each toast with 3 slices of roast beef, a spoonful or two of rémoulade, and a heap of fried onions. Sprinkle with parsley and serve.

CRANBERRY UPSIDE-DOWN TOAST

Serves 4

Part French toast, part upside-down cake, this toast is all decadence, and is an excellent use for day-old bread you might have lingering in the kitchen. You can make the topping with just about any fruit—tart cranberries are gorgeous, especially for the holidays, but pineapple, apples, pears, and quince are excellent too.

Six ¾-inch (2 cm) thick slices day-old country-style bread, brioche, or challah
5 tablespoons (115 g) unsalted butter, softened, plus extra for the bread
⅔ cup (150 g) packed light brown sugar
⅔ cup (65 g) pecan halves

1½ cups (150 g) fresh or frozen cranberries
½ cup (120 ml) heavy (double) cream
2 egg yolks
1 tablespoon granulated sugar
1 teaspoon vanilla extract
⅛ teaspoon kosher (coarse) salt

1. If your bread slices are long and can't easily fit in a 9-inch (23 cm) cake pan or baking dish, then slice them in half on an angle (this will depend on the type of bread you're using).

2. Preheat the broiler (grill) to high. Toast the bread according to the broiler instructions on page 7. Set the bread aside.

3. Preheat the oven to 375°F (190°C/Gas Mark 5).

4. In a small bowl, stir together the butter and brown sugar until smooth and creamy. Coat the bottom of a 9-inch (23 cm) round cake pan or square baking dish with the butter-sugar mixture. Add the pecans, rounded side down, then add the cranberries on top.

5. In a shallow bowl, whisk together the cream, egg yolks, granulated sugar, vanilla, and salt. Dip the toasts in the cream mixture so they are well saturated on both sides. Arrange the toasts in the cake pan, squeezing them in together in an even layer. Spoon any remaining cream mixture over the bread slices. Bake until the top of the toast is crisp around the edges and dry all the way across the surface, and the cranberries have burst, 20–25 minutes.

6. Remove the pan from the oven, cool 5 minutes, then carefully invert it onto a large plate. Break the toast apart into pieces and serve.

LEMONGRASS KIWI TOAST WITH HONEY CREAM

Fresh and verdant kiwi is like light therapy during the bleak colorscape of winter. A quick lemongrass syrup (see the Burnt Sugar and Coconut Ice Cream Toast, page 113) lifts kiwi's brightness even more. I love this for dessert paired with honey-sweetened whipped cream spiked with Greek yogurt for a tart touch. For breakfast, kill the whipped cream; just use the yogurt or crème fraîche with a drizzle of honey and top it with granola instead of the toasted poppy seeds.

KIWI

4 kiwis, peeled and cut into small pieces
1 tablespoon plus 1 teaspoon lemongrass syrup (page 113)

TOAST

Four ¾-inch (2 cm) thick slices country-style bread
Unsalted butter, softened, for the bread
⅓ cup (80 ml) heavy (double) cream
2 tablespoons honey
⅓ cup (80 ml) plain Greek yogurt
2 teaspoons poppy seeds

1. **Make the kiwi:** In a small bowl, stir together the kiwi and lemongrass syrup and set aside.

2. **Make the toast:** Toast the bread according to the instructions on pages 7–8, then set the toast aside to cool slightly.

3. Using a whisk or a stand mixer fitted with the whisk attachment (or a hand mixer), whip the cream to medium-stiff peaks. Add the honey and whisk to combine, then whisk in the yogurt.

4. In a small skillet (frying pan), toast the poppy seeds over medium heat until they taste a little nutty, 30 seconds–1 minute. Transfer to a small bowl.

5. To serve, top each toast with the kiwi. Cover each with a spoonful of the honey cream and sprinkle with poppy seeds.

SPICY LOBSTER BALCHAO TOAST

San Francisco | Serves 4

Balchao is a Portuguese-inspired recipe from the state of Goa, on India's west coast. It is made with white wine vinegar, chiles, and tomatoes—all New World ingredients that made their way to India via explorers and colonization. Suvir Saran, chef at American Masala in San Francisco, adds pan-seared, chile-marinated lobster tails to the sauce for a sophisticated spin, making this a beautiful addition to any holiday menu. It packs quite a bit of heat—so sensitive palates, be forewarned!

BALCHAO

2 lobster tails (about 1 lb/455 g in shells), halved lengthwise
Juice of ½ lemon or lime
2 teaspoons kosher (coarse) salt
¼ teaspoon cayenne pepper
1½ tablespoons canola (rapeseed) oil
6 fresh curry leaves, roughly torn (optional)
3 dried red chiles
¾ teaspoon cumin seeds
2 spicy fresh green chiles (such as serrano or Thai chiles), very finely chopped (seeded for less heat)
1 red onion, finely chopped
1½ teaspoons sugar
1½ teaspoons white wine vinegar
¾ cup (180 ml) canned (tinned) chopped tomatoes
2 tablespoons heavy (double) cream
1 tablespoon (15 g) unsalted butter

1. **Make the balchao:** Place the lobster tails on a large plate. In a small bowl, stir together the lemon juice, 1 teaspoon of the salt, and the cayenne. Spoon the mixture over the cut sides of each lob-ster tail. Refrigerate while you make the sauce.

2. In a medium saucepan wide enough to hold 4 lobster tail halves in a single layer, combine the oil, curry leaves, dried chiles, and cumin seeds and

TOAST

Four ¾-inch (2 cm) thick slices bread (preferably brioche)
Unsalted butter, softened, for the bread

cook over medium-high heat, stirring often, until the cumin browns, about 2 minutes. Stir in the green chiles and when they start to brown, after about 1 minute, add the onion and remaining 1 teaspoon salt. Cook, stirring often, until the onion is sticky and brown, 7–10 minutes (if the onion starts to stick to the pan, splash it with a few tablespoons of water, stirring and scraping up any browned bits). Stir in the sugar and vinegar, cook for 1 minute, then stir in the tomatoes and cook until the sauce is jammy, about 4 minutes.

3. Put the lobster tails cut side down in the sauce, and cook until the meat is opaque, 5–6 minutes. Trans-fer the tails to a plate and pop the meat out from the shells. Add the cream and butter to the sauce, return the lobster meat to the pan, and cook gently for another 1–2 minutes, until the tails are warmed through. Remove from the heat.

4. **Make the toast:** Toast the bread according to the instructions on pages 7–8. To serve, top each toast with a lobster tail half and cover with sauce.

BEEF MINCE ON TOAST

London | Serves 4

Through his London restaurant, St. John, Fergus Henderson had a seismic impact on chefs worldwide making offal like kidneys and tongues, hooves and glands cool again. For this toast, he uses reserved drippings and pan juices from a roast to soak into the toast, then tops the lot with a slow-cooked ground beef mince made with carrots, leeks, and onion. Though he says that omitting peas could cause a massive gastronomic row for beef mince traditionalists, he does it anyhow—and then, just to cause even more trouble, Henderson adds wine to the mince as well!

BEEF MINCE

1 tablespoon extra-virgin olive oil
1 medium yellow onion, halved and thinly sliced
1 medium leek, white and light green part only, halved lengthwise and thinly sliced crosswise
1 medium carrot, halved lengthwise and thinly sliced crosswise
4 garlic cloves, finely chopped
2 pounds (910 g) ground (minced) chuck (20% fat)
2 canned whole plum tomatoes or ¼ cup (60 ml) canned (tinned) chopped tomatoes
⅓ cup (30 g) rolled oats
2 tablespoons Worcestershire sauce
1½ cups (355 ml) dry red wine
¼–½ cup (60–120 ml) chicken stock or broth (optional)
1 teaspoon fine sea salt
½ teaspoon freshly ground black pepper

1. **Make the beef mince:** In a large skillet (frying pan), heat the oil over medium-high heat for 2 minutes. Reduce the heat to medium, add the onion, leek, carrot, and garlic, and cook, stirring often, until the onion is soft, 5–6 minutes. Crumble the beef into the pan and stir to mix it into the vegetables and break up the meat. Cook, stirring often, until the beef loses its pink color, 8–10 minutes. Crush the whole tomatoes in your hand and over the

TOAST

Four ¾-inch (2 cm) thick slices Pullman loaf or wheat bread
4 tablespoons (¼ cup) beef drippings or pan sauce from a roast (or softened butter, in a pinch)
Finely chopped fresh flat-leaf parsley (optional)

pan. While stirring, add the oats, followed by the Worcestershire sauce, and finally the wine. The sauce should be loose and thick (like lava); if the sauce is too thick, add enough chicken stock to make it lava-like. Stir in the salt and pepper, reduce the heat to low, and cook, stirring occasionally and adding stock if the pan goes dry, until the mixture looks rich and creamy and the fat sepa-ates out from the meat and rests at the surface of the mince, 1½–2 hours.

2. **Make the toast:** Toast the bread according to the instructions on pages 7–8. If you used the broiler (grill) method, leave the broiler on. Other-wise, position an oven rack in the upper third of the oven and preheat the broiler to high. Spread the beef drippings over one side of each slice, then place the toast on a foil-lined baking sheet and broil until bubbling, 1–2 minutes. Serve with the mince spooned over the toast and finish with parsley, if desired.

SPRING

67 PARM BUTTER, FRIED EGG, AND ASPARAGUS TOAST

68 RAMP PESTO ON TOAST WITH BURRATA AND PEPPADEWS

71 CUMIN-ROASTED CARROTS AND MUHAMMARA TOAST

72 SWEET SHRIMP AND FAVA SMASH TOAST

75 PICKLE-Y EGG SALAD TOAST

76 CHILI LAMB ON TOAST WITH HARISSA AIOLI

79 DANISH RYE MEATBALL TOAST WITH PICKLED CUCUMBERS

80 CHÈVRE AND STICKY MAPLE WALNUT TOAST

83 ROASTED STRAWBERRIES WITH ROSE-WHIPPED RICOTTA ON TOAST

84 ALMOND-ORANGE FLOWER TOAST

87 GUEST CHEF: DAN KLUGER'S MINTY PEA AND CHÈVRE TOAST

88 GUEST CHEF: ITAMAR SRULOVICH AND SARIT PACKER'S CHOPPED LIVER TOAST WITH ALEPPO PASTE AND CARAMELIZED ONION

PARM BUTTER, FRIED EGG, AND ASPARAGUS TOAST

Serves 4

A little Parmigiano-Reggiano cheese and garlic powder stirred into butter ups the ante for this breakfast toast (and it certainly could be breakfast-for-dinner). I prefer thick spears of asparagus to pencil-thin ones since they broil up with a silky interior. If you can only find thin asparagus, instead of broiling which can toughen them, toss them in a hot skillet with olive oil, salt, and pepper for a few minutes (shake the pan often), and you're good to go.

PARM BUTTER

3 tablespoons (45 g) unsalted butter, softened
¼ cup (60 g) finely grated Parmigiano-Reggiano cheese
¾ teaspoon garlic powder
¼ teaspoon kosher (coarse) salt

TOAST

12 asparagus spears, tough ends snapped off, spears halved on an angle
1 tablespoon extra-virgin olive oil
Kosher (coarse) salt
Freshly ground black pepper
Four ¾-inch (2 cm) thick slices rustic Italian bread
1 tablespoon (15 g) unsalted butter
4 eggs
Red pepper flakes, for serving
Flaky salt

1. **Make the parm butter:** In a small bowl, stir together the butter, Parmigiano-Reggiano, garlic powder, and salt until it forms a paste.

2. **Make the toast:** Position an oven rack in the top third of the oven and preheat the broiler (grill) to high. Line a rimmed baking sheet with foil.

3. Arrange the asparagus on the baking sheet, drizzle with the oil, and sprinkle with salt and pepper. Shake the pan to season the asparagus on all sides, then broil until tender, shaking the pan midway through broiling, 6–8 minutes total.

4. Spread each bread slice with the parm butter. Toast according to the broiler or toaster oven (mini oven) oven instructions on pages 7–8. Top each toast with asparagus.

5. In a large nonstick skillet (frying pan), melt the butter over medium-high heat. Fry the eggs in the butter until the whites are set and the yolks are still soft, 3–4 minutes. Set a fried egg over the asparagus on each toast. Sprinkle with red pepper flakes, a few pinches of flaky salt, and a few grinds of black pepper.

RAMP PESTO ON TOAST WITH BURRATA AND PEPPADEWS

Serves 4 (with leftover pesto)

Garlicky spring ramps (wild leeks) make an insanely delicious pesto, an idea I first learned about from my friend, New York chef Matt Weingarten. Here, I use lightly roasted pistachios and microwave-dehydrated mint instead of the classic pesto duo of pine nuts and basil. Drying herbs in the microwave preserves their fresh flavor and retains more of their essence when compared to oven drying—the mint flavor here is subtle and elegant. With a jar of this pesto in your fridge, you can pretty much transform any "plain" dish into something really special—from scrambled eggs, to pasta, to a simple roast beef sandwich. If ramp season has passed you by, swap in half a pound (225 g) of scallions (spring onions).

RAMP PESTO

30 fresh mint leaves
½ cup (60 g) shelled pistachios
6 ounces (170 g) ramps, greens separated
  from the bulbs, roots trimmed
½ cup (120 g) finely grated Pecorino-Romano
  cheese
Finely grated zest of 1 lemon
1 teaspoon kosher (coarse) salt,
  plus more if needed
½ cup (120 ml) extra-virgin olive oil
½ lemon

TOAST

Four ¾-inch (2 cm) thick slices country-style bread
Extra-virgin olive oil, for the bread,
  plus extra for serving
Flaky salt
Peppadew peppers, thinly sliced, for serving
8 ounces (225 g) burrata cheese

1. **Make the ramp pesto:** Preheat the oven to 350°F (180°C/Gas Mark 4). Spread the pistachios on a rimmed baking sheet and roast just until they get a slight gloss on the surface, 4–6 minutes. Remove from the oven and transfer to a medium plate to cool. While the pistachios toast, place the mint leaves in a single layer on a plate and microwave in 15-second increments until they become brittle and dry, 30 seconds–1 minute. Set aside to cool.

2. Transfer the ramps to a food processor along with the pecorino, microwave-dried mint, lemon zest, salt, and pistachios and pulse until roughly chopped.

With the motor running, begin to drizzle in the olive oil until the pesto is pretty smooth. Squeeze in the lemon juice and add more salt if needed.

3. **Make the toast:** Toast the bread according to the instructions on pages 7–8. To serve, slather a generous amount of the ramp pesto over each toast and top with a few slices of Peppadew peppers and a couple of pieces of burrata. Drizzle with more olive oil and sprinkle with more flaky salt.

CUMIN-ROASTED CARROTS AND MUHAMMARA TOAST

Serves 4 (with leftover muhamarra)

This toast is a homage to one from chef Dan Kluger (see his toast on page 87): a cumin-roasted carrot and avocado salad that took New York City by storm. Here, the carrots are roasted with cumin and honey and then heaped over *muhammara*, a tangy walnut spread made with sweet-tart pomegranate molasses. The leftover *muhammara* makes an excellent dip for veggies or chips.

CARROTS AND MUHAMARRA

6 medium carrots, halved lengthwise
3 tablespoons extra-virgin olive oil
1 tablespoon honey
1 teaspoon ground cumin
1½ teaspoons kosher (coarse) salt
2 large red bell peppers
1 garlic clove, unpeeled
1 cup (100 g) walnuts, toasted
1½ tablespoons pomegranate molasses
¼ teaspoon smoked paprika or hot paprika
¼ teaspoon freshly ground black pepper

TOAST

Four ¾-inch (2 cm) thick slices sesame seeded bread
Extra-virgin olive oil, for the bread
Flaky salt
½ lemon
Honey, for serving
2 tablespoons salted, roasted sunflower seeds
2 tablespoons finely chopped fresh mint leaves

1. **Make the carrots:** Position one oven rack in the upper third and a second in the lower third of the oven and preheat to 400°F (200°C/Gas Mark 6). Line a baking sheet with foil.

2. Arrange the carrots on the baking sheet and drizzle with 2 tablespoons of the olive oil and honey. Sprinkle with the cumin and ½ teaspoon salt and use your hands to roll the carrots around in the spices, making sure each carrot is evenly coated. Roast for 15 minutes. Shake the pan and roast until golden brown and tender, 10–15 minutes longer. Remove from the oven and set aside.

3. **Make the muhammara:** Preheat the broiler (grill) to high. Arrange the peppers and garlic on the same foil-lined baking sheet and broil on the upper rack, turning occasionally, until the peppers are charred and blackened on all sides and the garlic clove is golden brown, 12–15 minutes total. Transfer the vegetables to a medium bowl, cover well, and let steam for 20 minutes.

4. Once the peppers are cool enough to handle, peel off the skin and remove the stem and seeds. Peel the garlic and place the clove in a food processor along with the roasted peppers, walnuts, pomegranate molasses, the remaining 1 tablespoon of olive oil, remaining 1 teaspoon salt, paprika, and pepper. Pulse until well combined and chunky, five to six 1-second pulses.

5. **Make the toast:** Toast the bread according to the broiler instructions on page 7. To serve, spread each toast with a generous few spoonfuls of the *muhamarra* and top with a few carrots. Finish with a squeeze of lemon juice, a pinch of flaky salt, and a drizzle of honey. Sprinkle with the sunflower seeds and mint.

SWEET SHRIMP AND FAVA SMASH TOAST

Serves 4

Sweet and intensely verdant fava beans are the absolute essence of spring. True, they are a bit of work to shell and peel, but sometimes the best things in life require just a smidge of elbow grease. The sweetness of the smash is beautifully accented by sweet butter-poached shrimp (prawns) and licorice-tinged tarragon, though fresh mint works beautifully too. For a shortcut, try making the smash with frozen or fresh peas—no shelling required!

TARRAGON BUTTER AND FAVAS

4 tablespoons (60 g) unsalted butter, softened
1 tablespoon finely chopped fresh tarragon leaves
1¾ teaspoons plus a pinch of kosher (coarse) salt
8 ounces (225 g) shelled fava beans (from
  2–2½ pounds/910 g–1.1 kg favas in the pod)
1½ tablespoons extra-virgin olive oil
½ sweet onion (such as a Vidalia), finely chopped
2 tablespoons heavy (double) cream

TOAST

1 tablespoon (15 g) unsalted butter
½ pound (225 g) large shrimp (prawns), shelled,
  deveined, and halved lengthwise
Kosher (coarse) salt
Juice of ½ lemon
Four ¾-inch (2 cm) thick slices country-style bread
Flaky salt
A few handfuls of watercress or baby spinach

1. **Make the tarragon butter:** In a small bowl, mix together the butter, tarragon, and a pinch of kosher salt. Set aside.

2. **Make the favas:** Fill a small bowl with ice water and set aside. Bring a small saucepan of water to a boil. Add 1 teaspoon of the salt and the fava beans and blanch the favas for 1 minute. Drain and shock favas in the ice water. Once the favas are cool, use your finger and thumb to pinch and slip off the skins. Place the skinned favas in a small bowl. (If using peas instead of favas, skip this step entirely.)

3. In a medium skillet (frying pan), heat the oil over medium heat. Add the onion and ½ teaspoon of the salt and cook, stirring occasionally, until the onion is soft, 5–6 minutes. Stir in the fava beans and cook until they are tender, 3–5 minutes. Transfer the mixture to a food processor, add the cream, 1 tablespoon of the tarragon butter, and

the remaining ¼ teaspoon salt, and process until smooth.

4. **Make the toast:** In a medium skillet (frying pan), melt the butter over medium heat. Add the shrimp and cook slowly, spooning the butter over the shrimp, until they start to curl, about 1 minute. Season to taste with salt, turn the shrimp over and cook on the other side until they are cooked through, about 1 minute longer. Transfer to a medium bowl and toss with the lemon juice.

5. Spread the bread slices with the remaining tarragon butter and sprinkle with flaky salt. Toast according to the broiler, grill (barbecue), or toaster oven (mini oven) instructions on pages 7–8. To serve, top each toast with a generous amount of fava smash. Add the cress to the shrimp and toss to combine, then spoon it over the fava smash. Sprinkle with flaky salt.

PICKLE-Y EGG SALAD TOAST

Serves 4

A splash of pickle juice is the tweak that gives my egg salad its addictive umami-in-every-bite tastiness. I lean toward an egg salad with lots of bells and whistles like crunchy celery or radishes, fresh herbs, scallions, a smidge of Dijon, chopped cornichon pickles, and just enough mayonnaise to keep it creamy. I always squirrel some away for another snack or lunch with tortilla chips.

EGG SALAD

5 hard-boiled eggs, peeled and roughly chopped
3 tablespoons mayonnaise
¼ cup (60 ml) chopped cornichon pickles,
   plus 2 teaspoons pickle brine
2 scallions (spring onions), light green and
   white parts only, finely chopped
1 celery stalk, finely chopped
1 tablespoon finely chopped tender-leaf fresh
   herbs (such as basil, chervil, dill, parsley,
   or tarragon), plus a little extra for serving
½ teaspoon Dijon mustard
½ teaspoon kosher (coarse) salt
½ teaspoon freshly ground black pepper

TOAST

Four ¾-inch (2 cm) thick slices country-style bread
Extra-virgin olive oil, for the bread
Kosher (coarse) salt, for the bread
2 cups (60 g) baby lettuces or arugula (rocket)

1. **Make the egg salad:** Place the chopped eggs in a medium bowl. Add the mayonnaise and, using a fork, gently smash them together just enough so that the mayonnaise begins to get tinted by the yolks (you should still have plenty of larger pieces of egg white in the mix). Stir in the pickles and pickle brine, scallions, celery, herbs, mustard, salt, and pepper.

2. **Make the toast:** Toast the bread according to the instructions on pages 7–8. Let cool for a few minutes before topping. To serve, divide the salad greens among the toasts and top with egg salad and herbs.

CHILI LAMB ON TOAST WITH HARISSA AIOLI

Serves 4

When tied as a roast, leg of lamb is usually reserved for holidays and special occasions. If you untie the roast, you have a wonderfully lean, tender, and quick-cooking joint that's simple to make. As a toast, leg of lamb works beautifully sliced against the grain and elegantly settled over harissa aioli for a satisfying main dish. I usually cook the lamb under the broiler, but it's also fantastic grilled (barbecued).

CHILI SPICED LAMB

1 teaspoon chili powder
1 teaspoon sweet paprika
¾ teaspoon ground coriander
¾ teaspoon ground cumin
1 teaspoon kosher (coarse) salt
¼ teaspoon freshly ground black pepper
1 pound (455 g) boneless lamb steak or
   boneless leg of lamb, ¾–1-inch (2–2.5 cm) thick,
   trimmed of extra fat (if using leg of lamb, also
   trim the silverskin)
1 tablespoon honey
1 tablespoon ketchup
1 tablespoon canola (rapeseed) oil

TOAST

Four ¾-inch (2 cm) thick slices country-style bread
Extra-virgin olive oil, for the bread
Kosher (coarse) salt
½ cup (120 ml) mayonnaise
1 tablespoon harissa paste
2 tablespoons finely chopped fresh chives or
   scallions (spring onions)
Flaky salt

1. **Make the lamb:** In a small bowl, whisk together the chili powder, paprika, coriander, cumin, salt, and pepper. Rub the mixture all over the lamb, place the lamb on a foil-lined rimmed baking sheet, and set aside for 1 hour or refrigerate for up to overnight. In another small bowl, stir together the honey and ketchup and set aside.

2. Position an oven rack in the top third of the oven and preheat the broiler (grill) to high. Rub the lamb with the oil and broil until it is browned and charred, 6–7 minutes. Brush the browned side of the lamb with the honey-ketchup mixture and broil until it starts to sizzle, 30 seconds–1 minute. Turn the lamb over and broil the other side until the internal temperature at the thickest part reaches between 142°F and 145°F (61°C and 63°C) for medium-rare, 4–5 minutes longer. Brush the remaining honey-ketchup mixture over the top and broil until it starts to sizzle, 30 seconds–1 minute. Remove the lamb from the oven (leave the broiler on) and set it on a plate to rest for 10 minutes before slicing thinly against the grain at a sharp (45°) angle to the cutting (chopping) board. Toss the sliced lamb with any collected lamb juices.

3. **Make the toast:** Toast the bread according to the broiler, grill (barbecue), or toaster oven (mini oven) method on pages 7–8. In a small bowl, stir together the mayonnaise, harissa, and chives. To serve, spread each toast with the harissa aioli and layer the lamb on top. Sprinkle with flaky salt.

DANISH RYE MEATBALL TOAST WITH PICKLED CUCUMBERS

Serves 4 (with leftover meatballs and pickled cucumbers)

While Italian meatballs may be better known, Scandinavians love their meatballs too, especially on a slice of good rye bread with plenty of butter. This superbly rich Danish version gets an extra dose of hearty rye flavor from fresh rye breadcrumbs, a combo of ground pork and beef, fresh dill, and a wink of allspice. The Danes don't mess around when it comes to butter, so buy the best you can find and spread it on *thick*.

CUCUMBERS AND MEATBALLS

1 medium cucumber, thinly sliced crosswise
2¼ teaspoons kosher (coarse) salt
¼ teaspoon sugar
2 tablespoons distilled white vinegar
3 tablespoons finely chopped fresh dill
⅓ loaf rye bread (save the rest for the toast), cut into 1-inch (2.5 cm) cubes
¼ cup (60 ml) whole (full-fat) milk
1 egg
½ teaspoon freshly ground black pepper
Heaping ¼ teaspoon ground allspice
1 medium yellow onion, coarsely grated
1 small shallot, finely chopped
½ pound (225 g) ground (minced) sirloin (10% fat)
½ pound (225 g) ground (minced) pork
2 tablespoons (30 g) unsalted butter
2 tablespoons canola (rapeseed) oil

TOAST

Four ¾-inch (2 cm) thick slices rye bread
Unsalted butter, softened (preferably European-style cultured butter), for the bread
Flaky salt
Whole-grain Dijon mustard, for serving

1. **Make the cucumbers:** In a medium bowl, toss together the cucumbers, 1¼ teaspoons of the salt, sugar, vinegar, and 1 tablespoon of the dill. Cover well and refrigerate until serving.

2. **Make the meatballs:** In a food processor, pulverize the bread cubes into fine crumbs. Measure out 1 cup and set aside (freeze any remaining crumbs for another use).

3. In a large bowl, whisk together the milk, egg, pepper, allspice, and remaining 2 tablespoons dill and 1 teaspoon salt. Stir in the breadcrumbs, then stir in the onion and shallot. Crumble in the ground beef and pork. Mix together until well combined (the mixture will be wetter than traditional meatballs). Shape about 1½ tablespoons of the mixture into a loose, flattish ball. Set on a plate and repeat with the remaining mixture.

4. Line a plate with a paper towels and set aside. In a large heavy-bottomed skillet (frying pan), melt the butter over medium-high heat. Add the canola oil and about half of the meatballs to the pan. Reduce the heat to medium and cook the meatballs until browned, 3–4 minutes. Turn the meatballs over and brown the other side, 3–4 minutes longer. Transfer the meatballs to the towel-lined plate and repeat with the remaining meatballs.

5. **Make the toast:** Toast the bread according to the instructions on pages 7–8. To serve, sprinkle the toast with flaky salt, then give it a generous swipe of the mustard. Smash a few meatballs on top of each toast and serve with cucumber slices.

CHÈVRE AND STICKY MAPLE WALNUT TOAST

Serves 4 (with leftover sticky walnuts)

My friend Angela Miller runs the incredible Consider Bardwell cheese company in Vermont. I was at her farm on a very cold early-spring day when her first baby goat, Darius, was born. She nursed Darius with a tiny bottle filled with his mama's milk. It was right then that I understood the seasonality of chèvre: baby goat + milk-producing mama goat = plenty of goat's milk for chèvre. You can buy chèvre year-round, but once you consider the flush of babies that arrive in the spring, it just makes sense to eat chèvre as a seasonal treat.

STICKY WALNUTS

¾ cup (75 g) walnut halves
⅓ cup (80 ml) maple syrup
2 tablespoons light corn syrup (golden syrup)
¼ teaspoon anise seeds
Pinch of kosher (coarse) salt

TOAST

4 ounces (115 g) chèvre, at room temperature
3 tablespoons heavy (double) cream
Pinch of kosher (coarse) salt
Four ¾-inch (2 cm) thick slices fruit-and-nut bread
Unsalted butter, softened, for the bread
Flaky salt

1. **Make the sticky walnuts:** Position one oven rack in the top third and another in the middle of the oven and preheat to 400°F (200°C/Gas Mark 6). Arrange the walnuts on a rimmed baking sheet and toast on the lower oven rack until they are lightly golden, 7–8 minutes. Transfer to a plate to cool.

2. In a medium saucepan, combine the maple syrup, corn syrup, anise seeds, and salt and bring to a simmer over medium-high heat. Stir in the toasted walnuts, reduce the heat to medium-low, and gently simmer until the walnuts are well saturated, about 3 minutes. Remove from the heat and transfer the sticky walnuts to a heat-safe bowl. (The sticky walnuts can be made up to 1 week ahead and refrigerated; microwave to loosen them before serving.)

3. **Make the toast:** In a medium bowl, mash the chèvre with a fork. Mix in 1 tablespoon of the cream and once the chèvre is smooth, stir in the remaining 2 tablespoons cream and the kosher salt.

4. Toast the bread according to the instructions on pages 7–8. To serve, spread a generous amount of creamy chèvre over the buttered side of each piece of toast. Spoon a scoop or two of the sticky walnuts over the top and serve sprinkled with flaky salt.

ROASTED STRAWBERRIES WITH ROSE-WHIPPED RICOTTA ON TOAST

Serves 4

Roasting strawberries may seem counterintuitive, especially with sweet late-spring berries that beg to be devoured straight from the box. But subject them to hot oven heat and you'll get these intensely concentrated, jammy fruit bombs. Roasted strawberries are beautiful spooned over ricotta lightly whipped with heavy cream; and a splash of rose water adds a soft and ethereal floral quality.

STRAWBERRIES

4 cups (1 lb/455 g) strawberries, hulled and halved
2 tablespoons sugar

TOAST

1 cup (250 g) fresh ricotta cheese
¼ cup (60 ml) heavy (double) cream
1 tablespoon sugar
2 teaspoons rose water
Four ¾-inch (2 cm) thick slices rustic Italian bread
Unsalted butter, softened, for the bread
Kosher (coarse) salt

1. **Roast the strawberries:** Preheat the oven to 350°F (180°C/Gas Mark 4). Line a rimmed baking sheet with parchment paper.

2. In a bowl, toss together the strawberries and sugar. Arrange the strawberries cut side up on the baking sheet and roast until the strawberries are soft and juicy, about 20 minutes. Remove from the oven and return them to the bowl to cool. (The strawberries can made be up to 1 week ahead and refrigerated.)

3. **Make the toast:** In a medium bowl, vigorously whisk together the ricotta, cream, sugar, and rose water until the mixture is smooth and holds soft peaks, about 30 seconds.

4. Toast the bread according to the instructions on pages 7–8. Let the toast cool slightly before topping. Top each toast with ricotta cream and serve the strawberries and accumulated juices spooned over the top.

ALMOND-ORANGE FLOWER TOAST

Serves 4

Do you know bostock? It's an almond and orange flower syrup–soaked slice of brioche, topped with almond cream, and baked until browned, puffed, and gorgeous. If you like almond croissants, you'll go crazy for bostock. The softly floral tone comes from a syrup made using orange flower water, a little almond extract, and fresh orange zest buzzed into the almond cream to create a rich and custard-like topping. You'll have some leftover syrup on hand; save it to mix into maple syrup to top pancakes or waffles.

ALMOND CREAM

1½ cups (145 g) unsalted almonds
  (preferably skinned)
⅓ cup (70 g) sugar
3 tablespoons (45 g) unsalted butter, softened
1 egg
Finely grated zest of 1 orange
½ teaspoon almond extract
½ teaspoon kosher (coarse) salt

TOAST

½ cup (100 g) sugar
1 tablespoon honey
1½ tablespoons orange flower water
Four ¾-inch (2 cm) thick slices day-old brioche
  or challah
3 tablespoons (45 g) unsalted butter, softened
4 tablespoons (¼ cup) sliced (flaked) almonds
Confectioners' (icing) sugar, for serving

1. **Make the almond cream:** In a food processor, finely grind the almonds. Add the sugar, butter, egg, orange zest, almond extract, and salt and process until creamy and smooth.

2. **Make the toast:** In a small saucepan, combine ½ cup (120 ml) water, the sugar, and honey and bring to a simmer. Stir occasionally until the sugar is dissolved, remove from the heat, and set aside to cool. Add the orange flower water.

3. Preheat the oven to 400°F (200°C/Gas Mark 6).

4. Spread one side of the bread slices with the butter, then brush with the orange flower syrup. Use a spoon to liberally dollop and spread a layer of almond cream ¼-inch (0.5 cm) thick onto each slice. Place on a baking sheet, sprinkle 1 table-spoon almonds over each, and bake until the topping is browned, 12–15 minutes. Remove from the oven and let cool slightly, then serve showered with confectioners' sugar.

MINTY PEA AND CHÈVRE TOAST

New York City | Serves 4 (with leftover mint oil and minty peas)

Dan Kluger popularized the toast concept at the white-hot Manhattan restaurant ABC Kitchen. His kabocha squash and ricotta toast was one of the most rhapsodized dishes in the New York City food scene, in many ways sparking the toast trend on the East Coast. Here, Kluger turns to spring toast via a jalapeño-spiked minty pea mash. The garlic is blanched several times in simmering water, a chef trick to soften the sharpness of raw garlic.

MASHED PEAS

1 garlic clove, peeled but left whole
2 cups (40 g) fresh mint leaves
1 cup (240 ml) extra-virgin olive oil
1 tablespoon plus ¼ teaspoon kosher (coarse) salt
Pinch of sugar
2 cups (290 g) peas (preferably fresh)
½ jalapeño chile, finely chopped (seeded for less heat)

TOAST

Four ½-inch (1.25 cm) thick slices country-style bread
Extra-virgin olive oil for the bread, plus extra for serving
4 ounces (115 g) fresh chèvre, at room temperature
Finely grated zest of ½ lemon
Flaky salt and freshly ground black pepper

1. **Make the mashed peas:** Place the garlic in a small saucepan, cover with cold water, and bring to a boil. Drain and re-cover with cold water. Bring to a boil again, drain, and repeat one more time. Transfer the garlic to a blender.

2. Fill a medium bowl with ice water and set aside. Fill the saucepan with cold water, bring to a boil, and add the mint leaves. Blanch the mint for 10 seconds, then use a slotted spoon to transfer the mint to the ice water. Scoop out of the ice water (keep the bowl of water) and squeeze the cooled mint in a few paper towels to wring out any extra moisture. Add the mint to the garlic along with the olive oil. Blend until very smooth, then pour the mint oil into a small bowl and set the bowl into the ice water bath to chill (make sure the ice water doesn't get into the oil); this ensures the mint oil will stay bright green.

3. Fill another bowl with ice water and set aside. Fill the saucepan with cold water and bring to a boil. Add 1 tablespoon of the salt, the sugar, and peas and cook until the peas are bright green and rise to the surface (taste one—it should be sweet, not starchy), about 2 minutes. Drain the peas and transfer them to the ice water to chill, then scoop the peas out onto a tea towel to drain.

4. Measure out ¼ cup (60 ml) of the peas and set aside. Transfer the remainder to the blender and add ¼ cup (60 ml) of the mint oil, the jalapeño, and the remaining ¼ teaspoon salt. Pulse until the mixture is rough in texture. Transfer to a medium bowl and stir in the reserved whole peas.

5. **Make the toast:** Toast the bread using the pan-frying method on page 8. To serve, spread each toast with chèvre. Top with the pea mash, lemon zest, flaky salt, and pepper. Drizzle with some olive oil.

CHOPPED LIVER TOAST WITH ALEPPO PASTE AND CARAMELIZED ONION

London | Serves 4 (with leftover chopped liver)

At Honey & Co. (an Israeli street-food-meets-home-cooking diner in London), chef-owners and husband-and-wife team Itamar Srulovich and Sarit Packer bring a taste of Israel and the Middle East to London's Fitzrovia neighborhood. The Ottolenghi alums share a recipe for chopped liver on toast spiced with Aleppo chile paste and some cumin. Though the vibe is a blend of Eastern European and North African, the finish is old-school Jewish deli–style all the way. This recipe makes enough chopped liver to serve a crowd.

CHICKEN LIVERS

2 tablespoons (30 g) unsalted butter
2 tablespoons vegetable oil
1 large yellow onion, halved and thinly sliced
1½ teaspoons kosher (coarse) salt
1 pound (455 g) chicken livers, trimmed of extra fat and patted dry
¼ teaspoon freshly ground black pepper
1½ tablespoons ground cumin
2 tablespoons Aleppo chile paste (or harissa paste)
Juice of 1 lemon

TOAST

Four ¾-inch (2 cm) thick slices Pullman loaf
Unsalted butter, softened, for the bread
2 radishes, thinly sliced
Baby lettuce leaves
1 hard-boiled egg, peeled and thinly sliced

1. **Make the chicken livers:** In a large skillet (frying pan), melt 1 tablespoon of the butter over medium-high heat. Add 1 tablespoon of the oil and heat together for 1 minute. Add the onion and ¼ teaspoon of the salt and cook, stirring often, until the onion softens, 3–4 minutes. Reduce the heat to medium-low and cook, stirring occasionally, until the onion is very dark brown, 15–20 minutes longer. Transfer the onion to a medium bowl.

2. Season the chicken livers with ¼ teaspoon of the salt and the pepper. Add the remaining 1 table-spoon each butter and oil to the skillet and set it over high heat. Once the butter is melted, add the chicken livers and cook, stirring occasionally, until the exterior of the liver turns opaque, 4–5 minutes. Sprinkle the liver with the cumin, stir, then add the chile paste and lemon juice. Cook until the livers are just pink in the middle (not red or bloody), 2–3 minutes longer. Stir in the onion and mix to combine. Transfer the liver-onion mixture to the bowl, cover, and refrigerate until well chilled, at least 2 hours.

3. Turn the chilled liver and onions onto a cutting (chopping) board and roughly chop to combine. Return the mixture to the bowl and stir in the remaining 1 teaspoon salt.

4. **Make the toast:** Toast the bread according to the instructions on pages 7–8. To serve, spoon some chopped liver on top of each toast. Finish with lettuce leaves, a few radish slices, and egg slices.

SUMMER

93   GRILLED CORN AND SCALLION TOAST WITH CILANTRO CREMA

94   TOMATO BUTTER TARTINE

97   AVOCADO FATTOUSH TOAST

98   BANH MI SCHMEAR TOAST

101   FRIED EGGPLANT CON TOMATE ON TOAST

102   ITALIAN PLUM CONSERVA, GORGONZOLA, AND DUCK CONFIT TOAST

105   POACHED CHICKEN SALAD TOAST WITH PEACHES

106   CRAB AND AVOCADO TOAST

109   GRILLED STEAKHOUSE HANGER TOAST

110   HAZELNUT S'MORE TOAST

113   BURNT SUGAR AND COCONUT ICE CREAM TOAST

114   GUEST CHEF: ANDREW FEINBERG'S EGGPLANT, SWEET PEPPER, AND CAPER TOAST

117   GUEST CHEF: BILL GRANGER'S TUNA MELT TOAST WITH OLIVE SALSA

GRILLED CORN AND SCALLION TOAST WITH CILANTRO CREMA

Serves 4

Lanky and charred, grilled scallions are easy to make and look so stunning heaped in a tangle on top of bread. Cilantro crema, whirled in a food processor with plenty of lime and jalapeño, cushions the scallions; and smoky grilled corn, sliced off the cob adds sweetness and crunch. Crumbly Mexican Cotija cheese punctuates the toast with a salty bite; if you can't find it, swap in ricotta salata or feta.

CREMA, CORN, AND SCALLIONS

½ cup (120 ml) sour cream
4 tablespoons (¼ cup) fresh cilantro (coriander) leaves
¼ cup (40 g) crumbled Cotija cheese
½ jalapeño chile, roughly chopped (seeded for less heat)
Juice of 1 lime
½ teaspoon kosher (coarse) salt
4 teaspoons extra-virgin olive oil
8 scallions (spring onions), ends trimmed
½ teaspoon kosher (coarse) salt
2 ears fresh corn, shucked

TOAST

Four ¾-inch (2 cm) thick slices country-style bread
3 tablespoons extra-virgin olive oil
2 radishes, thinly sliced
½ cup (80 g) crumbled Cotija cheese
1 lime, quartered
1 teaspoon cayenne pepper

1. **Make the cilantro crema:** In a food processor, pulse the sour cream, cilantro, Cotija, jalapeño, lime juice, and salt to a smooth puree. Transfer to a small bowl, cover, and refrigerate.

2. **Cook the scallions and corn:** Heat a grill (barbecue) or grill pan (griddle) to high. Drizzle 2 teaspoons of the oil over the scallions, sprinkle with ¼ teaspoon of the salt, and cook on both sides until charred and soft, 4–5 minutes. Transfer to a plate. Brush the remaining 2 teaspoons oil over the corn, season with the remaining ¼ teaspoon salt, and cook on all sides until the kernels are golden brown and slightly charred, 6–8 minutes. When the corn is cool enough to handle, slice the kernels off the cob.

3. **Make the toast:** Drizzle the bread slices with the olive oil. Toast according to the grilling (barbecuing) method on page 8. Top each toast with some crema and corn, add 2 scallions, then finish with the radishes and Cotija. Dip one side of each lime wedge in the cayenne, squeeze over the toast, and serve.

TOMATO BUTTER TARTINE

Serves 4 (with leftover tomato butter)

At the height of the season, the tomatoes at the greenmarket are impossible to resist, all lined up on a table just begging to be squeezed ever so gently. No matter how carefully I pack them, a few tomatoes always seem to get crushed at the bottom of my bag. Making tomato butter out of sautéed tomatoes and good butter is a great use for those half-squished guys, a trick I learned as the food editor at Tasting Table. A pinch of Piment d'Espelette, a slightly smoky roughly ground red pepper from the Basque country, or sesame-seaweed salt, like Japanese *furikake*, is tasty sprinkled over the top.

TOMATO BUTTER

1 tablespoon extra-virgin olive oil
1 large tomato, cored and chopped into ½–¾-inch (1.25–2 cm) chunks
½ teaspoon kosher (coarse) salt
8 ounces (225 g) unsalted butter, softened

TOAST

Four ¾-inch (2 cm) thick slices country-style bread
Extra-virgin olive oil, for the bread
Kosher (coarse) salt, for the bread
3 large radishes, thinly sliced
Flaky salt
Piment d'Espelette or furikake (optional)

---

1. **Make the tomato butter:** In a large nonstick skillet (frying pan), heat the olive oil over medium-high heat. Add the tomatoes and salt, reduce the heat to medium-low, and cook, stirring and pressing on the tomatoes occasionally, until the tomatoes are thick and pasty and the liquid has evaporated, 20–25 minutes. Transfer the tomato paste to a plate and set aside to cool completely.

2. Scrape the cooled tomato paste into a blender (or a medium bowl if using an immersion blender), add the butter, and blend until smooth (a few flecks of tomato skin are pretty). Transfer the butter to a large sheet of parchment paper and roll it into a

12-inch (30 cm) log, or pack the butter into 1 or 2 ramekins and cover with plastic wrap.

3. **Make the toast:** Toast the bread according to the instructions on pages 7–8. Let the toast cool completely.

4. To serve, spread each toast with a good amount of tomato butter, then shingle the radishes on top. Sprinkle with flaky salt and, if desired, Piment d'Espelette or *furikake*. The remaining butter can be wrapped in plastic wrap and rolled into a log; it will last in the fridge for up to 2 weeks or in the freezer for up to 3 months.

AVOCADO FATTOUSH TOAST

Serves 4

Avocado toast is the Holy Grail of toast. It's the one usually served at toast-friendly cafés and is perhaps *the* most popular toast made at home. I one-up this classic avocado toast pairing—avocado with juicy tomato slices—by turning the duo into fattoush, a genius Middle Eastern salad made with tomatoes, onion, parsley, and cucumber interspersed with toasty pita chips and sumac (here, the toast acts as the crisp pita bits). Za'atar, a Middle Eastern sesame-and-dried herb-seasoning, and black nigella seeds, which have an almost oniony appeal, are also delicious tossed into the salad. Look for all three seasonings—sumac, za'atar, and nigella—in Middle Eastern markets, specialty food stores, or online.

FATTOUSH

½ small red onion, finely chopped
½ teaspoon plus a few pinches of kosher (coarse) salt
2 juicy medium tomatoes, cored and finely chopped
1 medium cucumber, peeled, seeded, and finely chopped
3 radishes, thinly sliced
½ fresh red chile (such as a Thai bird's-eye chile or a Fresno), halved and thinly sliced crosswise
2 tablespoons roughly chopped fresh flat-leaf parsley
1 tablespoon extra-virgin olive oil
Juice of 1 lemon
½ teaspoon ground sumac

TOAST

Four ¾-inch (2 cm) thick slices country-style bread
Extra-virgin olive oil, for the bread
Kosher (coarse) salt, for the bread
1 avocado, quartered, pit discarded
Za'atar
Nigella seeds (optional)

1. **Make the fattoush:** Sprinkle the red onion with a few pinches of salt and set aside (the salt helps to dull its sharpness). In a medium bowl, toss together the tomatoes, cucumber, radishes, chile, parsley, olive oil, lemon juice, sumac, and the remaining ½ teaspoon salt.

2. **Make the toast:** Toast the bread according to the instructions on pages 7–8. Let the toast cool slightly before topping.

3. Smash one-quarter of the avocado over each toast. Stir the salted red onion into the fattoush, then spoon a few generous scoops over the avocado. Add a few spoonfuls of the collected juices, too. Serve sprinkled with za'atar and nigella, if desired.

BANH MI SCHMEAR TOAST

Serves 4 (with leftover pickled vegetables)

You may beg to differ, but I think the best part of a Vietnamese *banh mi* sandwich is the toppings: the pickled carrots, slightly bitter daikon, fresh cilantro, and jolting-hot jalapeño slices. Take all of this and buzz it with some cream cheese and you have a killer toast topping. The toast is great with just the topping, or with some nice bagel fixings for a full-on Sunday brunch toast. I like smoked trout, capers, and onions—and, when in season, slices of tomato are spot-on awesome. The fish sauce adds a happy hit of umami, but if it's really not your thing, swap in some pickle juice and a squeeze of lemon.

PICKLED·VEGETABLE TOPPING

2 tablespoons rice vinegar
1½ tablespoons fish sauce (or equal parts pickle juice and lemon juice)
⅛ teaspoon sugar (about 2 small pinches)
Pinch of kosher (coarse) salt
2 medium carrots, sliced lengthwise into ribbons using a vegetable peeler
1 medium daikon (about 4 oz/115 g), peeled and sliced lengthwise into ribbons using a vegetable peeler
1 medium jalapeño chile, thinly sliced crosswise (seeded for less heat)
1 cup (8 oz/230 g) cream cheese
4 tablespoons (¼ cup) fresh cilantro (coriander) leaves

TOAST

Four ¾-inch (2 cm) thick slices baguette
Grapeseed oil, for the bread
Kosher (coarse) salt
Thinly sliced cucumber (optional)
Sliced tomato (optional)
Smoked trout, flaked into shards (optional)
Thinly sliced red onion (optional)
Capers, rinsed (optional)

1. **Make the pickled-vegetable topping:** In a medium bowl, whisk together the vinegar, fish sauce, sugar, and salt until the sugar and salt dissolve. Add the carrots, daikon, and jalapeño slices and stir to sub-merge. Cover the bowl and refrigerate for at least 1 hour and up to 2 days.

2. Remove the vegetables from the pickling liquid (reserve the liquid) and place them on a few paper towels to drain, then transfer to a food processor. Add the cream cheese and cilantro, and pulse until everything is well combined (you want the schmear to have some texture). Add a little of the pickling liquid for extra tang or to thin the mixture out and ease processing, if needed.

3. **Make the toast:** Toast the bread according to the instructions on pages 7–8. Let cool for a few minutes before topping. To serve, spread each toast with some schmear and finish with the fixing(s) of your choice.

FRIED EGGPLANT CON TOMATE ON TOAST

Serves 4

Bread seasoned with olive oil and garlic and rubbed with fresh tomato: This is *pan con tomate*, a thrifty Spanish invention originally intended to stretch out one tomato to serve many people. Now, *pan con tomate* is one of the highlights of Spanish tapas. To make the toast more substantial so it can stand in as a meal, I drive it through Italy and top it with a fried eggplant slice and some fresh basil, almost an ode to eggplant parmigiana. For a more decadent toast, top it with a slice of fresh mozzarella and then broil until molten.

FRIED EGGPLANT

1 medium eggplant (aubergine)
  (about 1 lb/455 g), sliced lengthwise into slabs
  ¼-inch (0.5 cm) thick
1½ teaspoons kosher (coarse) salt
⅓ cup (40 g) all-purpose (plain) flour
⅓ cup (50 g) fine cornmeal
¼ cup (60 g) finely grated Pecorino-Romano cheese
¼ teaspoon freshly ground black pepper
½ cup (120 ml) grapeseed oil
¼ cup (60 ml) extra-virgin olive oil

1. **Make the fried eggplant:** Place the eggplant on a rimmed baking sheet. Using 1 teaspoon of the salt, sprinkle both sides of the eggplant. Set aside for 20 minutes.

2. In a shallow bowl, combine the flour, cornmeal, pecorino, remaining ½ teaspoon salt, and the pepper.

3. In a large heavy-bottomed skillet (frying pan), heat the grapeseed and olive oils over medium-high heat. Dredge 4 slices of eggplant through the flour mixture, making sure both sides are nicely coated, and lightly tap off any excess. Carefully slide them into the oil and fry until browned on both sides, 6–8 minutes total. Transfer to a plate lined with paper towels and repeat with the remaining eggplant.

TOAST

3 garlic cloves, peeled and smashed
3 tablespoons extra-virgin olive oil
Four ¾-inch (2 cm) thick slices country-style bread
Flaky salt
1 tomato, halved horizontally
A handful of thinly sliced fresh basil leaves

4. **Make the toast:** Place the garlic and olive oil in a small microwave-safe bowl. Microwave on high for 30 seconds, swirl, then microwave for another 30 seconds. Set the bowl aside to let the garlic infuse the oil. (Or warm the garlic and olive oil in a small saucepan over medium-low heat, swirling until it is fragrant, 2–3 minutes. Remove from the heat and let the oil infuse and cool.)

5. Drizzle the bread slices with the garlic oil and sprinkle with flaky salt. Toast according to the broiler or grilling (barbecuing) instructions on pages 7–8. Remove the toast from the oven and rub the cut side of the tomato over each slice, squeezing the half over the bread until you are left with mostly pulp and skin (each tomato half should about cover 2 toasts). To serve, lay a piece of eggplant over each piece of toast and sprinkle with basil and flaky salt.

ITALIAN PLUM CONSERVA, GORGONZOLA, AND DUCK CONFIT TOAST

Serves 4 (with leftover conserva)

Making duck confit is a time-consuming process, so I buy mine ready-made at my local specialty food store. If you can't find duck confit, swap in duck or pork rillettes (a happy medium between the meat of confited duck legs and pâté), pâté, or even shredded roast chicken. A *conserva* is like jam with the addition of large pieces of fruit and nuts. This one gets a subtle Asian bend from five-spice powder, a blend that includes star anise and cardamom among other heady additions.

PLUM CONSERVA

1 pound (455 g) plums (preferably Italian prune plums), pitted and chopped
½ cup (80 g) dried cherries
½ cup (60 g) chopped walnuts
Juice of ½ lemon
¾ cup plus 1 tablespoon (165 g) sugar
½ teaspoon five-spice powder
Pinch of kosher (coarse) salt

TOAST

Four ¾-inch (2 cm) thick slices nut-and-fruit bread
Unsalted butter, softened, for the bread
Flaky salt
4 ounces (115 g) Gorgonzola dolce cheese
1 confited duck leg, skin removed, meat shredded
½ cup (15 g) baby arugula (rocket) leaves, roughly chopped

1. **Make the plum conserva:** In a medium saucepan, combine the plums, dried cherries, walnuts, lemon juice, and ½ cup (120 ml) water. Bring the liquid to a boil, stirring occasionally. Reduce the heat to medium and simmer, stirring often, until the plums break down, 4–5 minutes. Stir in the sugar, five-spice powder, and salt. Reduce the heat to medium-low and cook until the *conserva* is thick and glossy (or until you can draw a line with your finger across the back of a wooden spoon and the line doesn't fill in), 8–10 minutes longer. Remove from the heat and let cool, then transfer to an airtight container and refrigerate for up to 2 weeks.

2. **Make the toast:** Toast the bread according to the instructions on pages 7–8. To serve, spread each toast with the Gorgonzola and then with 1 or 2 generous spoonfuls of the *conserva*. Top with the shredded duck and arugula.

POACHED CHICKEN SALAD TOAST WITH PEACHES

Serves 4

Light, bright, and delicately balanced, this chicken salad arranged on toast feels much more elegant than your usual mayo-and-celery-heavy deli special. Poaching chicken breasts yields immensely tender meat, and as a bonus, the poaching liquid can be saved and used as chicken stock for another meal. If you can't find Fresno chiles (also called red jalapeños), substitute a green jalapeño or, to keep the red color, a couple of pinches of ground Aleppo chile.

POACHED CHICKEN SALAD

4 cups (950 ml) chicken broth or stock
3 sprigs fresh flat-leaf parsley
2 teaspoons coriander seeds
1 teaspoon fennel seeds
1 teaspoon black peppercorns
2 pounds (910 g) bone-in, skin-on chicken
   breasts (about 2 large breasts)
2 tablespoons extra-virgin olive oil
1½ tablespoons mayonnaise
1½ teaspoons whole-grain Dijon mustard
1 teaspoon kosher (coarse) salt, plus more if needed
¼ teaspoon freshly ground black pepper
¼ teaspoon ground cumin
¼ teaspoon ground coriander
1 large peach, unpeeled, finely chopped
1 fresh red or green chile (such as a Fresno,
   Thai bird's-eye chile, or a jalapeño), finely
   chopped (seeded for less heat)
12 fresh basil leaves, finely chopped

TOAST

Four ¾-inch (2 cm) thick slices country-style bread
Extra-virgin olive oil, for the bread
Kosher (coarse) salt, for the bread

1. **Make the poached chicken salad:** In a deep, wide, and straight-sided pan or large saucepan, bring the chicken broth, parsley sprigs, coriander seeds, fennel seeds, and peppercorns to a simmer over medium-high heat. Add the chicken. (The braising liquid should just cover the meat. If it doesn't, add just enough water to cover.) Reduce the heat to low and gently poach the chicken for 20 minutes. Steam should rise from the surface of the liquid, but you don't want to see any bubbles. Remove from the heat and let the chicken sit in the poaching liquid until both are close to room temperature, about 30 minutes. Remove the chicken from the poaching liquid and discard the skin. Shred the chicken into long strands (discard the bones). Place the chicken in a medium bowl and let cool completely.

2. In a small bowl, whisk together the olive oil, mayonnaise, mustard, salt, pepper, cumin, and ground coriander. Add the dressing to the chicken and using your hands, toss to combine, making sure all the chicken gets coated. Taste and adjust the salt if needed. Add the peach, chile, and basil, and toss to combine.

3. **Make the toast:** Toast the bread according to the instructions on pages 7–8. To serve, top each toast with chicken salad.

CRAB AND AVOCADO TOAST

Serves 4

Avocado on toast is a total phenomenon (see page 97), so here's another way to make it: *guasacaca*. A popular South American smooth-and-tangy guacamole hybrid, *guasacaca* is made by blitzing avocados with tomatillo salsa. Shards of sweet crab meat, a little mayo, a squeeze of lemon, and a pinch of salt easily turn a wonderfully breezy avocado toast into a fast and perfect summer meal.

GUASACACA

1 avocado, halved, pit discarded
Juice of ½ lime
4 tablespoons (¼ cup) tomatillo salsa
¼ teaspoon kosher (coarse) salt,
  plus more if needed

TOAST

6 ounces (170 g) crabmeat (preferably jumbo
  lump), drained and picked free of shells
4 tablespoons (¼ cup) finely chopped fresh
  cilantro (coriander) leaves
1 scallion (spring onion), light green and
  white parts only, finely chopped
2 teaspoons mayonnaise
¼ teaspoon kosher (coarse) salt, plus more as
  needed
Four ¾-inch (2 cm) thick slices rustic bread
Extra-virgin olive oil, for the bread

1. **Make the guasacaca:** In a blender, combine the avocado, lime juice, salsa, and salt and pulse until mostly puréed. (Or you can smash the avocado, then stir in the lime juice, salsa, and salt for a chunkier version.) Taste and add more salt if needed.

2. **Make the toast:** Set the crab meat in a medium bowl and using your fingers, fluff it into shards.

Add the cilantro, scallion, mayonnaise, and salt and use a fork to gently combine the ingredients, doing your best not to break up the crab meat into tiny bits.

3. Toast the bread according to the instructions on pages 7–8. To serve, top each toast with *guasacaca* and crab meat.

GRILLED STEAKHOUSE HANGER TOAST

Serves 4

Big on flavor and short on cooking time, hanger steak is my go-to inexpensive steak. Since there is only one hanger steak to a cow, some meat departments don't carry them; if you have trouble sourcing a hanger, you can use a flank steak or a skirt steak instead. A flank tends to be a bit thicker than a hanger, so it might take longer to cook, while a skirt often cooks up more quickly and needs precooking trimming to keep it lean. The spinach is enclosed in a foil bundle and cooked right on the grill; the heat from the grill wilts the spinach just enough so it can be spooned on top of the toast, making this marriage of steak and spinach *that* much more irresistible.

STEAK AND SPINACH

1 pound (455 g) hanger steak, trimmed of extra fat
3 medium garlic cloves, finely chopped
1 tablespoon plus 1 teaspoon kosher (coarse) salt
2 teaspoons freshly ground black pepper
8 cups (240 g) baby spinach, roughly chopped
1 tablespoon (15 g) unsalted butter,
   cut into small pieces
1 tablespoon finely chopped fresh chives
2 tablespoons heavy (double) cream
2 tablespoons grapeseed oil

1. **Make the steak:** Rub the steak with the garlic, 1 tablespoon of the salt, and the pepper. Refrigerate for 1 hour or overnight. Remove the steak from the refrigerator 1 hour before cooking.

2. **Make the spinach:** Preheat one side of a gas grill (barbecue) to medium-high and the other side to medium. (Or prepare a charcoal grill so the coals are banked more on one side than the other; you should be able to hold your hand 5 inches (13 cm) above the grate for 3–4 seconds on the medium-high side and 4–5 seconds on the medium side.) Set a large piece of foil on a work surface and mound the spinach just left of the middle. Dot the spinach with the butter and add the chives, cream, and remaining salt. Fold the right side of the foil over so the ends meet, then crimp and fold the foil to make a tight seal all the way around.

TOAST

Four ¾-inch (2 cm) thick slices country-style bread
3 tablespoons extra-virgin olive oil
Flaky salt

3. Use tongs to dip a folded paper towel in the oil, then use the oiled towel to grease the grill grates. Place the steak on the hot side of the grill and the spinach on the medium-hot side. Grill the steak on both sides until it is charred, 2–3 minutes per side. Move the steak to the medium-hot side of the grill and cook it for an additional 2–3 minutes for medium-rare (the steak will yield to light pressure in its thickest part). Set the steak aside. Remove the spinach from the grill.

4. **Make the toast:** Drizzle the bread slices with the olive oil and sprinkle with salt. Toast according to the grilling (barbecuing) method on page 8. Open up the foil packet and divide the spinach and accumulated juices among the pieces of toast. Slice the steak against the grain and on an angle to the cutting (chopping) board. Arrange the steak slices over the spinach. Sprinkle with flaky salt and serve drizzled with accumulated meat juices from the cutting board.

HAZELNUT
S'MORE TOAST

Serves 4 (with leftover chocolate-hazelnut spread)

I daresay that summer without a s'more is not summer at all. Even if you're not the type who's into campfires and starlit cookouts, you can still reap the rewards of gooey marshmallow-chocolate bliss by taking s'mores indoors. Instead of a chocolate bar, try this homemade chocolate-hazelnut spread on toast—it's over-the-top luscious (and even great without the marshmallows). Char the bread, so you get that marshmallow-on-fire magic. You'll have about 1½ cups (355 ml) of leftover chocolate-hazelnut spread. I have no doubt you'll find loads of ways to eat it.

CHOCOLATE-HAZELNUT SPREAD

1¼ cups (175 g) hazelnuts (preferably already skinned)
2 tablespoons sugar
2 tablespoons honey
2 tablespoons confectioners' (icing) sugar
2 tablespoons canola (rapeseed) oil
¾ teaspoon flaky salt
½ pound (225 g) best-quality semisweet (dark) chocolate (greater than 60% cacao), finely chopped and melted

1. **Make the chocolate-hazelnut spread:** Preheat the oven to 350°F (180°C/Gas Mark 4). Arrange the hazelnuts on a rimmed baking sheet and toast, shaking the pan halfway through roasting, until golden brown, 12–15 minutes. Transfer the hazelnuts to a heat-safe plate to cool. (If the hazelnuts are skin-on, wrap them in a tea towel, set aside for a minute, then use the towel to rub off the skins.) Once cool, transfer the nuts to a food processor and grind until they become a smooth paste, scraping down the bowl as needed, about 1–3 minutes.

2. Add the sugar, honey, confectioners' sugar, oil, and salt to the nut butter and blend until combined. Add the melted chocolate and process until

TOAST

Four ¾-inch (2 cm) thick slices rustic bread
3 tablespoons (45 g) unsalted butter, softened
Flaky salt
16 marshmallows, quartered

combined, then scrape the mixture into an airtight container and leave out at room temperature to thicken for about 3 hours or overnight. (The spread can be refrigerated after 1 day for up to 2 weeks; let it sit out at room temperature for at least 30 minutes before using so it returns to a spreadable consistency. Note that after refrigerating, the texture will be less smooth.)

3. **Make the toast:** Spread the bread slices with the butter and sprinkle with salt. Toast according to the broiler instructions on page 7. Remove from the broiler (grill) and swipe some chocolate-hazelnut spread over each slice. Top with a handful of marshmallows. Position an oven rack in the top third of the oven, then return the baking sheet to the broiler. Broil the toasts until the marshmallows are golden brown, 15–30 seconds (watch the marshmallows closely as broiler intensities vary). Let cool for 1–2 minutes before serving.

BURNT SUGAR AND COCONUT ICE CREAM TOAST

Serves 4

Welcome to your new addiction: buttered, toasted bread, dunked in lemongrass syrup, dipped in sugar, singed in butter until the sugar shellacs itself to the bread like a sweet veneer, and then topped with ice cream and toasted coconut. Think of it as a sundae–French toast mash-up with the glistening sugar topcoat of a crème brûlée to finish.

LEMONGRASS SYRUP

2 fresh lemongrass stalks
½ cup (100 g) sugar

TOAST

½ cup (50 g) unsweetened (desiccated) coconut flakes or shredded coconut
Four ¾-inch (2 cm) thick slices country-style bread or brioche
3 tablespoons (45 g) unsalted butter, softened
3 tablespoons sugar
1 pint (about 500 ml) coconut ice cream

1. **Make the lemongrass syrup:** Place the lemongrass on a cutting (chopping) board and cut away the root end and the tops. Peel away the thick and dry outer layers to expose the tender reed. Using the back of a chef's knife, smash the lemongrass, then cut the reed crosswise into several 3-inch (7.5 cm) lengths (you should smell the essential oils).

2. In a small saucepan, combine the smashed lemongrass with the sugar and ½ cup (120 ml) water. Simmer over medium heat, stirring occasionally, until the sugar is dissolved. Simmer 4 minutes longer to infuse the syrup with lemongrass. Remove from the heat and set aside to cool; discard the lemongrass. (The syrup can be made a few weeks ahead and refrigerated.)

3. **Make the toast:** Preheat the oven to 350°F (180°C/ Gas Mark 4). Spread the coconut on a rimmed baking sheet and toast in the oven, stirring occasionally, until golden around the edges, 6–8 minutes. Transfer to a plate and set aside.

4. Spread the bread slices with the butter. Toast according to the pan-frying method on page 8, using a large nonstick skillet (frying pan). Transfer the toast to a plate but keep the skillet at the ready.

5. Pour the lemongrass syrup into a wide and shallow bowl. Spread the sugar out on a medium plate. Dip one side of each piece of toast in the lemongrass syrup for a few seconds to saturate. Transfer the toast, syrup side down, to the plate with the sugar, and press down on the bread to get a nice sugar coating. Return the toast to the skillet, sugared side down. Repeat with the remaining toast. Cook over medium heat until the sugared side is browned and caramelized, about 2 minutes.

6. Divide the toast among 4 plates, sugared side up. To serve, top with 1 or 2 scoops of ice cream, a drizzle of lemongrass syrup, and a sprinkle of toasted coconut.

EGGPLANT, SWEET PEPPER, AND CAPER TOAST

Brooklyn, NY | Serves 4

Andrew Feinberg is the chef-owner of Franny's in Brooklyn, which, while renowned for its pizzas, is perhaps better known as *the* restaurant that initiated the raw kale salad world domination. Here, Feinberg, inspired by a dish he ate in Naples, combines sautéed sweet peppers with an Apulian-style eggplant purée.

EGGPLANT, PEPPERS, AND CAPERS

1 large eggplant (aubergine) (about 1¼ pounds/
  570 g), peeled and sliced crosswise into rounds
  ¾-inch (2 cm) thick
1½ teaspoons kosher (coarse) salt,
  plus more as needed
¾ cup plus 3 tablespoons (225 ml) extra-virgin
  olive oil, plus extra for the pan
5 medium garlic cloves, roughly chopped
2 anchovy fillets
1 tablespoon fresh oregano or marjoram leaves
5 teaspoons late-harvest agrodolce wine vinegar
  (or half white balsamic and half red wine vinegar)
Freshly ground black pepper
2 red bell peppers, cut into 1-inch (2.5 cm) pieces
4 tablespoons (¼ cup) salt-packed capers, rinsed

1. **Make the eggplant:** Set the oven to 400°F (200°C/
Gas Mark 6). Grease a rimmed baking sheet.

2. Sprinkle the eggplant with ½ teaspoon of the salt and toss with 3 tablespoons of the olive oil. Arrange on the baking sheet and roast until the bottoms are browned, 15–20 minutes. Flip and cook until fork-tender, about 15 minutes longer. Transfer the eggplant to a plate and set aside.

3. In a medium skillet (frying pan), heat ½ cup of the olive oil, the garlic, and anchovies, and cook over medium heat just until the oil begins to bubble,

TOAST

Four ¾-inch (2 cm) thick slices country-style bread
Extra-virgin olive oil, for the bread,
  plus extra for serving

2–3 minutes. Remove from the heat and swirl in the oregano and 1 teaspoon of the vinegar. Set aside.

4. Purée the eggplant in a food processor until smooth. Add the cooled garlic-anchovy oil and ½ teaspoon of the salt and process until smooth. Season with black pepper.

5. **Make the peppers and capers:** In a large skillet (frying pan), heat the remaining 5 tablespoons (⅓ cup) olive oil over high heat. Add the peppers and once they start to brown, after 3–4 minutes, reduce the heat to medium-high and stir in the remaining salt. Cook, stirring occasionally, until the peppers blister, about 10 minutes. Add the capers and cook until they are crisp, 4–5 minutes. Remove from the heat, stir in the remaining 4 teaspoons vinegar, and season with pepper.

6. **Make the toast:** Toast the bread according to the instructions on pages 7–8. To serve, spread each toast with a thick layer of eggplant. Top with the pepper-caper mixture and drizzle with olive oil.

TUNA MELT TOAST WITH OLIVE SALSA

Sydney, Australia | Serves 4

I'm always curious about what chefs make in their home kitchens when they're starving. A bowl of cereal? Scrambled eggs? Doctored ramen? This toast is from Bill Granger, the chef-owner of nearly a dozen restaurants in Australia, Japan, the United Kingdom, South Korea, and Hawaii. He loves the tuna melt toast straight from the oven while the cheese is still lovely and oozy, and says that it's way better (and faster!) than even dialing for pizza.

OLIVE SALSA AND TUNA

1 small bunch fresh flat-leaf parsley, chopped
3 scallions (spring onions), light green and white parts only, finely chopped
¼ cup (35 g) pitted green olives (preferably Lucques), roughly chopped
1 tablespoon extra-virgin olive oil
Juice of ½ lemon
Kosher (coarse) salt (optional)
8 ounces (225 g) oil-packed canned (tinned) tuna, drained and flaked
4 marinated artichoke hearts, drained and thinly sliced
Heaping ¼ cup (about 35 g) shredded fresh mozzarella cheese (preferably buffalo mozzarella)
Scant ¼ cup (25 g) grated mozzarella cheese (not fresh mozzarella)
1 teaspoon freshly ground black pepper

TOAST

Four ¾-inch (2 cm) thick slices sourdough bread
Pinch of red pepper flakes

1. **Make the olive salsa and tuna:** In a small bowl, mix together the parsley, scallions, olives, olive oil, and lemon juice. Taste and season with salt if needed. In a separate bowl, stir together the tuna, artichokes, both mozzarellas, and black pepper until everything is evenly mixed.

2. **Make the toast:** Preheat the broiler (grill) to high. Arrange the bread on a foil-lined rimmed baking sheet. Toast the bread lightly on both sides, 1–2 minutes per side, until golden brown. Top each toast with the tuna mixture and sprinkle with some red pepper flakes. Broil until the cheese is melted and bubbling on top, 2–3 minutes. Serve hot, topped with the salsa.

Index

A

Acheson, Hugh
Hakurei turnips, poached chicken, and apple butter toast **34** 35
aleppo paste and caramelized onion, chopped liver toast with 88 **89**
almond-orange flower toast 84 **85**
apples
Dutch apple pie toast **30** 31
artichokes
three-cheese spinach-artichoke toast **48** 49
asparagus toast, Parm butter, fried egg, and **66** 67
aubergine see **eggplant**
avocado
avocado fattoush toast **96** 97
crab and avocado toast 106 **107**

B

bacon, lentil, and cabbage toast **44** 45
balchao toast, spicy lobster, **60** 61
banh mi schmear toast 98 **99**
beef
beef mince on toast 62 **63**
grilled steakhouse hanger toast **108** 109
patty melt toast **52** 53
roast beef, rémoulade, and fried onions smørrebrød 54 **55**
beets, roasted, on toast with labneh and saffron honey **40** 41
Bombay bubble and squeak toast 46 **47**
bread, basics 9
burgers
patty melt toast **52** 53
burnt sugar and coconut ice cream toast **112** 113
burrata and Peppadews, ramp pesto on toast with 68 **69**
butter
macadamia-cardamom butter 12
Parm butter 67
pepperoni butter 15
tomato butter 94
butternut squash
cider-glazed squash with

Manchego and spiced pecans 20 **21**

C

cabbage
Bombay bubble and squeak toast 46 **47**
lentil, bacon, and cabbage toast **44** 45
carrots, cumin-roasted, and muhammara toast **70** 71
cauliflower and beer rarebit toast 32 **33**
cheese
cauliflower and beer rarebit toast 32 **33**
cheesy pepperoni butter toast **14** 15
chèvre and sticky maple walnut toast 80 **71**
croque monsieur toast **18** 19
grilled corn and scallion toast with cilantro crema **92** 93
Italian plum conserva, Gorgonzola dolce, and duck confit toast 102 **103**
minty pea and chèvre toast **86** 87
patty melt toast **52** 53
ramp pesto on toast with burrata and Peppadews 68 **69**
roasted tomato and feta cream toast 50 **51**
three-cheese spinach-artichoke toast **48** 49
chèvre and sticky maple walnut toast 80 **71**
chicken
chopped liver toast with aleppo paste and caramelized onion 88 **89**
Hakurei turnips, poached chicken, and apple butter toast **34** 35
poached chicken salad toast with peaches **104** 105
sesame and honey-barbecue fried chicken toast 24 **25**
chili lamb on toast with harissa aioli 76 **77**
chopped liver toast with aleppo paste and caramelized onion 88 **89**
cider-glazed squash with Manchego and spiced pecans 20 **21**

cinnamon toast, best 38 **39**
coconut ice cream toast, burnt sugar and **112** 113
corn, grilled, and scallion toast with cilantro crema **92** 93
crab and avocado toast 106 **107**
cranberry upside-down toast **56** 57
croque monsieur toast **18** 19
cucumbers, pickled, Danish rye meatball toast with **78** 79

D

duck confit toast, Italian plum conserva, Gorgonzola dolce, and 102 **103**
Dutch apple pie toast **30** 31

E

eggplant (aubergine)
eggplant, sweet pepper, and caper toast 114 **115**
fried eggplant con tomate on toast **100** 101
eggs
Parm butter, fried egg, and asparagus toast **66** 67
pickle-y egg salad toast **74** 75

F

fattoush, avocado, toast **96** 97
fava beans
sweet shrimp and fava smash toast 72 **73**
Feinberg, Andrew
eggplant, sweet pepper, and caper toast 114 **115**
figs
maple pear toast with fig-sesame jam and balsamic drizzle 28 **29**

G

goat cheese
chèvre and sticky maple walnut toast 80 **71**
minty pea and chèvre toast **86** 87
Gorgonzola dolce, Italian plum conserva, and duck confit toast 102 **103**
Granger, Bill
tuna melt toast with olive salsa **116** 117
grilled corn and scallion toast

with cilantro crema **92** 93
grilled steakhouse hanger toast
    108 109

H
Hakurei turnips, poached chicken,
    and apple butter toast **34** 35
hazelnut s'more toast 110 **111**
Henderson, Fergus
    beef mince on toast 62 **63**

I
ice cream, coconut, burnt sugar
    and, toast **112** 113
Italian plum conserva, Gorgonzola
    dolce, and duck confit toast
    102 **103**

K
kiwi
    lemongrass kiwi toast with
    honey cream 58 **59**
Kluger, Dan
    cumin-roasted carrots and
    muhammara toast **70** 71
    minty pea and chèvre toast
    86 87

L
labneh and saffron honey, roasted
    beets on toast with **40** 41
lamb, chili, on toast with harissa
    aioli 76 **77**
lemongrass
    lemongrass kiwi toast with
    honey cream 58 **59**
    lemongrass syrup 113
lentil, bacon, and cabbage toast
    44 45
lobster, spicy, balchao toast **60** 61

M
macadamia-cardamom butter
    toast 12 **13**
maple pear toast with fig-sesame
    jam and balsamic drizzle 28 **29**
meatball toast, Danish rye, with
    pickled cucumbers **78** 79
muhammara toast, cumin-roasted
    carrots and **70** 71
mushroom, wild, forest toast **22** 23
mustard greens, garlicky, romesco
    toast with 16 **17**

O
olive salsa, tuna melt toast with
    116 117
onions
    chopped liver toast with aleppo
    paste and caramelized onion
    88 **89**
    roast beef, rémoulade, and
    fried onions smørrebrød 54 **55**

P
Packer, Sarit
    chopped liver toast with
    aleppo paste and
    caramelized onion 88 **89**
Parm butter, fried egg, and
    asparagus toast **66** 67
patty melt toast **52** 53
peaches, poached chicken
    salad toast with **104** 105
pears
    maple pear toast with fig-
    sesame jam and balsamic
    drizzle 28 **29**
    pea, minty, and chèvre toast **86** 87
pecans, spiced, cider-glazed
    squash with Manchego and 20 **21**
pepperoni butter, cheesy, toast **14** 15
peppers, bell
    eggplant, sweet pepper, and
    caper toast 114 **115**
cumin-roasted carrots and
    muhammara toast **70** 71
Perelman, Deb
    cauliflower and beer rarebit
    toast 32 **33**
pickle-y egg salad toast **74** 75
plums
    Italian plum conserva,
    Gorgonzola dolce, and duck
    confit toast 102 **103**
potatoes
    Bombay bubble and squeak
    toast 46 **47**
    smashed Tot and egg toast
    42 **43**

R
ramp pesto on toast with burrata
    and Peppadews 68 **69**
ricotta, rose-whipped on toast,
    roasted strawberries with **82** 83
roast beef, rémoulade, and fried

onions smørrebrød 54 **55**
romesco toast with garlicky
    mustard greens 16 **17**

S
s'more toast, hazelnut 110 **111**
sesame and honey-barbecue
    fried chicken toast 24 **25**
shrimp, sweet, and fava smash
    toast 72 **73**
spicy lobster balchao toast **60** 61
spinach
    grilled steakhouse hanger
    toast **108** 109
    three-cheese spinach-
    artichoke toast **48** 49
Saran, Suvir
    spicy lobster balchao toast
    60 61
Srulovich, Itamar
    chopped liver toast with
    aleppo paste and
    caramelized onion 88 **89**
strawberries, roasted, with rose-
    whipped ricotta on toast **82** 83

T
Tater Tots
    smashed Tot and egg toast 42 **43**
Thanksgiving toast **26** 27
three-cheese spinach-artichoke
    toast **48** 49
toasting, primer 7
tomatoes
    avocado fattoush toast **96** 97
    roasted tomato and feta
    cream toast 50 **51**
    romesco toast with garlicky
    mustard greens 16 **17**
    tomato butter tartine 94 **95**
tuna melt toast with olive salsa
    116 117
turkey
    Thanksgiving toast **26** 27
turnips, Hakurei, poached chicken,
    and apple butter toast **34** 35

W
walnuts
    chèvre and sticky maple
    walnut toast 80 **71**
    sticky walnuts 80
wild mushroom forest toast **22** 23

Author's Acknowledgments

A toast to everyone behind *Toast*: To the chefs who contributed recipes to this book, you're all rock stars: Hugh Acheson, Andrew Feinberg, Bill Granger, Fergus Henderson, Dan Kluger, Sarit Packer, Deb Perelman, and Suvir Saran. To my merry band of recipe testers, thanks for being game: Jessica Battilana, Mike and Sandi Campo, Alexis DeBoschnek, Penny De Los Santos, Kristin Donnelly, Lucille Fiore, Gabriella Gershenson, Sara Kate Gillingham, JJ Goode, Posie Harwood, Scott Hocker, Jonathan Kauffman, Debbie Manka, Denise Mickelson, Karen Palmer, Mike Pelzel, Adam Ried, Michelle Sayre (and crew), Joanne Smart, Stacey Watson, and Izabela Wojcik.

Evan Sung, photographer extraordinaire, food stylist Suzanne Lenzer, and prop stylist Maya Rossi: Thanks for making these toasts so sexy.

My agents, David Black and Sarah Smith: Your tenacity and dedication are above and beyond, and your wisdom far-reaching.

To my team at Phaidon, I am honored to have *Toast* on your list, grazie to: Commissioning Editor, Emily Takoudes; Project Editor, Olga Massov; Publisher, Emilia Terragni; Creative Director, Julia Hasting; designer Stefanie Weigler of Triboro; and the entire global Phaidon team.

To those who inspire me to be my best: Matt Grady; Billie Dionne; Chuck and Char Sayre (and family); the Israelis (Miriam, Iris, Tali, Orit, and Shai); Adeena Sussman; Ratha Chaupoly; Jill Vegas; Patrick McKee; Melissa d'Arabian; Matt Weingarten.

Mom, thanks for being the worst cook on the planet and burning all the toast—I learned to cook as a means of survival. Dad, I love you and miss you every second of every day. I cannot even begin to thank you, most of all, but I hope you already know. L'chaim. Rhys and Julian, my boys: You're my life, my greatest joy, and will always be my grandest achievements.

PHAIDON PRESS LIMITED
REGENT'S WHARF
ALL SAINTS STREET
LONDON N1 9PA

PHAIDON PRESS INC.
65 BLEECKER STREET
NEW YORK, NY 10012

WWW.PHAIDON.COM

FIRST PUBLISHED 2015
© 2015 PHAIDON PRESS LIMITED

ISBN 978 0 7148 6955 1

A CIP CATALOGUE RECORD FOR THIS BOOK IS AVAILABLE FROM THE BRITISH LIBRARY AND THE LIBRARY OF CONGRESS.

COMMISSIONING EDITOR: EMILY TAKOUDES
PROJECT EDITORS: OLGA MASSOV,
LAURA LOESCH-QUINTIN
PRODUCTION CONTROLLERS: STEVE BRYANT,
VANESSA TODD-HOLMES
DESIGN: STEFANIE WEIGLER / TRIBORO

PRINTED IN CHINA